Four Midwestern Sisters' Christmas Book

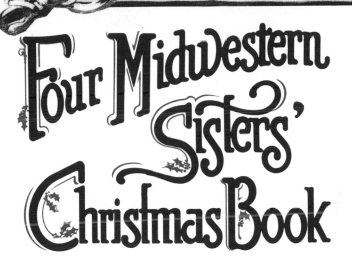

Four Midwestern Sisters' Christmas Book

Holly J. Burkhalter

with Kathy Lockard,
Karol Crosbie,
and Ruth Bosley

Illustrated by Richard Lillash

Viking

V I K I N G
Published by the Penguin Group
Viking Penguin, a division of Penguin Books USA Inc.,
375 Hudson Street, New York, New York 10014, U.S.A.
Penguin Books Ltd, 27 Wrights Lane, London W8 5TZ, England
Penguin Books Australia Ltd, Ringwood, Victoria, Australia
Penguin Books Canada Ltd, 10 Alcorn Avenue, Suite 300, Toronto, Ontario, Canada M4V 3B2
Penguin Books (N.Z.) Ltd, 182–190 Wairau Road, Auckland 10, New Zealand

Penguin Books Ltd, Registered Offices: Harmondsworth, Middlesex, England

First published in 1991 by Viking Penguin, a division of Penguin Books USA Inc.

1 3 5 7 9 10 8 6 4 2

Grateful acknowledgment is made for permission to
reprint the following copyrighted works:
Recipe for Grandma Jost's plain peppernuts reprinted by permission of Herald Press
from *Peppernuts: Plain and Fancy* by Norma Jost Voth. All rights reserved.
Excerpt from "Amahl and the Night Visitors" by Gian Carlo Menotti.
Copyright © 1951 (renewed) G. Schirmer, Inc. International copyright secured.
All rights reserved. Used by permission.
"The More It Snows" from *The House at Pooh Corner* by A. A. Milne. Copyright 1928
by E. P. Dutton, renewed © 1956 by A. A. Milne. Used by permission of
Dutton Children's Books, a division of Penguin Books USA Inc.

LIBRARY OF CONGRESS CATALOGING IN PUBLICATION DATA
Burkhalter, Holly.
Four midwestern sisters' Christmas book / Holly Burkhalter.
p. cm.
ISBN 0–670–83812–8
1. Burkhalter family.   2. Burkhalter, Holly — Family.
3. Christmas — Iowa — Ames.   4. Christmas — Middle West.   5. Ames
(Iowa) — Social life and customs.   6. Ames (Iowa) — Biography.
7. Middle West — Social life and customs.   I. Title.
CT274.B876B87 1991
929'.2'0973 — dc20   91–50166

Printed in the United States of America
Set in Cochin   Title handlettering by Richard Nebiolo
Designed by Amy Hill

When we were young, there were moments of such perfectly crystallized happiness that we stood stock still and silently promised ourselves that we would remember them always. And we did.

Contents

Four Midwestern Sisters' Christmas Book

Introduction

But it was good to think he had this to come back to, this place which was all his own, these things which were so glad to see him again and could always be counted upon for the same simple welcome.

— Kenneth Grahame,
The Wind in the Willows

Every Christmas our folks bring down from the attic a big cardboard star and install it in the upstairs bedroom window of the family home in Ames, Iowa. A light bulb hangs inside the star so when you round the corner at the end of the long drive home, you can see it shining there and you know it's Christmas. That star has been in the family for the past forty years, since Mom and Dad bought it for a dollar in Bluffton, Ohio. It isn't a very fancy thing, but Christmas wouldn't be Christmas without it.

We've been piling on holiday decorations and recipes and rituals ever since Mom and Dad got things going with the cardboard star. We four sisters decorate our own houses (in Ohio, Iowa, Illinois, and Washington, D.C.), give our own holiday parties, and experiment with recipes in our respective kitchens. But every year brings us all home again

1

for Christmas, to share our new discoveries with the family and to create more layers of family Christmas tradition.

Esprit de corps has always run strong in our family, but at Christmas it tends to run amok. Take the Christmas, probably around 1960, when we kids ranged in age from about five to mid-teens. In an excess of Christmas fellow feeling, Kathy made matching red and green plaid wool jumpers for Mom and the four of us sisters and matching vests for Dad and our brother, Gary. We wore our plaids in public, all seven of us, and formed an awesome sea of red and green. The plaid vests and jumpers were just one more family Christmas inspiration that made us feel part of an enchanted circle.

The jumpers are long gone, but all the rest of our Christmas traditions are intact. They remind us that things don't have to change. Christmas carols sound the same as they did when we were little. Mom has made fruitcake, and we're all home again for the holidays, just like always. It's Christmas, and you can count on it.

As young readers like to know "how people look," we will take this moment to give them a little sketch of the four sisters, who sat knitting away in the twilight, while the December snow fell quietly without, and the fire crackled cheerfully within.

—Louisa May Alcott,
Little Women

We don't knit. But like Meg, Jo, Beth, and Amy, we are each other's best pals, the same as when we were kids. In those days, it wasn't so much four sisters as it was two pairs, with brother Gary right smack in the middle. Kathy and Karol, the oldest in the family, were an unassailable partnership. And Ruth, the youngest—always called Roo by the family, after Baby Roo in *Winnie the Pooh*—and I were constant comrades.

The alliance of sister pairs deepened at Christmas. We were in our own worlds, bursting with secrets and plans. The older girls sewed Christmas presents in the heavily guarded seclusion of their bedroom, now off-limits to the rest of us. Roo and I retaliated with our own mysteries: One year we secretly rehearsed a two-sister Christmas pageant, complete with Roo as the Little Drummer Boy, pacing up and down in rubber boots and beating a Quaker Oats box. Another time we made a shoebox crèche, with glued-on straw (scavenged from a hayride) and a cotton-clouded firmament. Its brown-painted cardboard walls never did dry, and smeared indelibly onto us every time we got near it.

Now that we're in our thirties and forties, the pairs have dissolved. We live in four different cities and we've gone completely separate ways in our careers, but it seems that the older we get, the more we have in common. We all love to cook and bake and decorate and entertain. It's as if our collective Christmas conspiracy has begun to spill over into the rest of the year.

At least once a year the four of us meet in Chicago or Cincinnati or Washington for a sisters' reunion. Usually it's a Christmas shopping trip in early December. We love being together on our own in the big city, still looking and sounding a lot alike and pleased as punch that we are sisters.

Kathy is a college accounting instructor and lives in Sycamore, Illinois, with her husband, Jim Lockard, who is a  university professor. When I was little I wanted to be just like big sister Kathy, so I learned to play the piano and sew because she did. She fills her house with homemade Christmas from the hand-crocheted lace snowflakes on the tree to the cross-stitched Nativity sampler. Every year she and Jim and their daughter, Katie, who's now nine, throw an enormous Christmas open house that is full of glitter and joy and wonderful food. Being the eldest, Kathy remembers the most about our Christmases at home, and this book is full of those memories.

Karol and her eleven-year-old son, Jonathan, live in Ames, Iowa. Since we all converge on Ames for the holidays, many of our meals and parties are at their house — which the children like because Karol is there to listen to them and laugh at their jokes, and a cat and a rowdy dog are there to romp with. It is Karol who stays up till all hours stuffing the kids' stockings, and Karol who organizes the sledding, caroling, and skating parties. She has her own public relations business, and is also a writer and publicist for a social service agency for drug- and alcohol-dependent teenagers.

The youngest of the sisters is Roo, who lives in Cincinnati, Ohio, with her husband, Larry Bosley, their four-year-old daughter, Maren, and their baby daughter, Jourdan. Roo is a free-lance graphic designer. She spends months searching for glorious and perfect presents for everybody, and the packages she wraps are works of art. She and Larry, who is also in graphic design, are the official historians of the holidays, taking hundreds of wonderful snapshots and sending them to the rest of us to remember it all by. (A month after Christmas, we receive a fat package of photos from Roo and Larry with an order form to choose the prints we want. We circulate it to each other in an incompetent round-robin, and along about July our Christmas photos arrive in the mail.)

When we were kids, our brother, Gary, navigated between the pairs of sisters, though he was most often Roo's and my buddy. Nowadays he works for an insurance company in Mason City, Iowa, and sings lead in a barbershop quartet. His kind and serene wife, Marsha, is an oasis of calm at our family gatherings. Their nineteen-year-old daughter, Erin, and son Nathan, aged seventeen, take virtual charge of the little kids during the holidays, including their seven-year-old sister, Holly Beth. Erin and Nathan can deal with everything from changing a baby's diaper to teaching Jonathan wrestling holds. We couldn't manage at all without them.

I moved to Washington, D.C., about twelve years ago, where I live with my husband, John Fitzpatrick, but I'm still an Iowan at heart. I am privileged to work for Human Rights Watch, an organization that monitors and promotes international human rights. Eccentric as it may seem, to me human rights work and a family Christmas book are logically connected. Women all over the world are trying to do what my sisters and I do. They are trying to create warmth and beauty for their families. They are trying to feed their children, build their homes, and celebrate their traditions and rituals. The world should let them. It's a human right.

This book is full of our grandmother, who died at the age of ninety-six in 1984. She and my grandfather were Mennonite missionaries in India for forty years, and Dad was born and grew up there. Our grandparents moved back to the States in the mid-1950s and were with us every Christmas. Christmas is when we miss them most.

Our parents, Holly and Larry Burkhalter, are the center of our family. Dad is a violist, performing and recording with the Ames Piano Quartet, based at Iowa State University. He rides his bike back and forth to the university with his viola strapped on the rack in back, and he plays like a million bucks. He is also a first-class photographer (capturing, for example, that delicious snapshot of the family in our plaids), and he draws and designs. Roo got those genes, clearly.

Mom taught English to decades of seventh-graders in Ohio and Iowa, teaching them to love books and words and ideas. And she still had time to teach us everything we know about baking and entertaining and Christmas. Now retired, she runs a Third World crafts store, whose proceeds help maintain income-generating projects for women around the world.

Kathy, Karol, Roo, and I collected recipes and stories and memories for this book, thinking we would make a gift of it to our mother. But we found that the recipes and traditions are really her gift to us. She taught us to love cooking, she gave us peanut brittle and fruitcake, she read stories, and wrapped presents, and kept secrets.

Let's just say this book is to thank her and to say, "We remember."

Remembering Snow

For several years—the happiest of our childhood—we lived at "the farm," an old house on acres of wooded land far outside the city limits of Columbus, Ohio. We had to haul drinking water from the city in ten-gallon milk cans because the well water on the place was sulfurously undrinkable. The sulfur content was so high, in fact, that the well actually exploded once, flinging the cistern cover skyward, demolishing a doghouse (mercifully uninhabited), and singeing off Dad's eyebrows.

But everything else about the farm was perfect. In Civil War days the house had been a stopover on the underground railroad. It had mysterious nooks and crannies, foot-thick brick walls, and five fireplaces. There was a ruined stone foundation from a burned-down barn, a long gravel lane lined with oak trees, a dozen willows, a water pump that didn't work, and a meadow.

It snowed thick and clean and quiet at the farm. We skated and slid on a frozen creek, and flopped down on pristine patches of snow to make snow angels. We brought bowls of clean snow into the kitchen, and Mom would sprinkle them with vanilla and sugar to make "snow ice cream." Nowadays, most snow in my town is polluted, what with hurrying footsteps, car exhaust fumes, and the sprinkles of urban dogs. But the next time there is a snowstorm in Washington, I'm going to stand outdoors holding a big mixing bowl to catch the flakes so I can make snow ice cream, like we had at the farm.

We had a smiling German shepherd dog named Pokey, who galloped through the drifts, gulping snowflakes. We built snow forts and igloos, trying to make them Pokey-proof, because she would fling herself into them, bringing snowball mortar crashing down on top of herself. Bright cardinals and blue jays and squirrels swooped and chattered, and the branches of the pine trees grew heavy with snow frosting. In my memory it was like a Christmas card.

We had the grandest sledding parties in those days. Dad would trudge up and down the best hills, stomping his feet and dragging a piece of tin to pack down a trail. We sped down "suicide hill" countless times, the little girls sandwiched, shrieking, between Gary and the older sisters. Hearing the yells, Pokey tried to rescue us. She would hang on to our scarves and coats with her teeth, trying to keep us from hurtling down the hill.

The more it snows
(Tiddely pom),
The more it goes
(Tiddely pom),
The more it goes
(Tiddely pom),
On snowing.
And nobody knows
(Tiddely pom),
How cold my toes
(Tiddely pom),
How cold my toes
(Tiddely pom),
Are growing.

—A. A. Milne,
The House at Pooh Corner

Sometimes Dad would attach a long chain to the back of our 1954 two-tone green Plymouth and pull the five of us on a toboggan along the deserted back country roads. Decades later, this sounds unthinkably dangerous. In the country in those days, though, there were no other cars on the roads, and Dad kept the Plymouth down to a crawl.

Once during an enormous snowstorm the family's other car (barely a car, actually—it was a tiny, tubercular English Austin) got stuck in the snow at the bottom of the lane. We all bundled up and joyously pushed it out of the drifts. Afterwards Mom pronounced it a "snow day" and we all stayed home from school. One cold winter Sunday, the Plymouth gave up the ghost. There wasn't any question about whether we were going to church. We were. Dad conducted the church choir, and adopted a distinctly "show must go on" approach towards the crisis. It took several tries, but ultimately we loaded into the little Austin, all seven of us (with the littlest actually wedged against the ceiling), and drove in to town for church. The weary Austin looked like the clown car in the circus as, one after the other, we scrambled forth, dressed in our best and laughing our heads off.

We had bonfires and nighttime sledding parties under the winter stars. And when we clambered inside to get warm, we would find Mom working in the kitchen. In those days she wore a housedress and an apron, white socks and red oxford shoes, and she looked great. She would have just pulled a loaf of whole-wheat bread out of the oven. We'd have a piece right then and there, hot, with butter melting on it.

Whole-Wheat Bread

Makes two loaves

1 cup water
2 packages active dry yeast
1 cup buttermilk
3 tablespoons melted butter
3½ to 4 cups all-purpose white flour

1 tablespoon salt
¼ cup honey
¼ cup molasses
2 cups whole-wheat flour

Heat ½ cup of the water until very warm, about 115 degrees. Dissolve the yeast in the warm water. Let stand 5 minutes.

Heat the buttermilk, butter, and remaining ½ cup water until warm. Add this to the yeast mixture, along with 2 cups of the white flour. Beat with an electric mixer for 2 to 3 minutes.

Add the salt, honey, molasses, and 1 to 1½ cups white flour. Beat well. Gradually add the whole-wheat flour. (At some point, your mixer will give out. Carry on with a wooden spoon.) Knead for 8 to 10 minutes, adding white flour as needed, until the dough is smooth and satiny.

Place the dough in a greased bowl, and turn it over so the top surface is greased. Let rise, covered with a tea towel, until doubled in bulk (about 1½ hours). Punch down, divide in half, and let rest for 5 minutes. Form into loaves and place in two greased bread pans (8½ by 4 by 3 inches). Cover with a tea towel and let rise in a warm place until the dough has risen about 1 inch above the pans (about 1 hour).

Preheat oven to 375 degrees, and bake bread for 35 to 45 minutes. Remove from the pans, and cool on a wire rack.

Mom loves to bake, and she taught us to love it too. When we lived at the farm, before she started teaching, she baked nearly every day—pies and rolls and cookies. Ungrateful wretches that we were, we became so accustomed

to the joys of home-baked cookies that we thought the rarely purchased store-bought varieties were utterly exotic. It was misguided wonder; they were no competition for Mom's molasses crinkles, snickerdoodles, and chocolate chippers.

Mom drew the line, however, on the question of boxed cake mixes. She never made a single one, and we were taught to be snooty about the superiority of baked-from-scratch cakes. All but Roo, who, at the age of four, was easily corrupted. That Christmas, Mom and Dad bought her a toy bake set, complete with boxed mixes for brownies and yellow sheet cake and tiny mixing bowls, pans, cooling racks, spatulas, and spoons. Stirring, whipping, and spreading with rapturous abandon, Roo produced a miniature yellow baked object. It was a cake, sort of, and utterly tasteless and ugly. But Roo was in heaven, so we didn't tell her.

Mom always baked something special for our Wednesday night ritual. Every Wednesday after school, she drove us into the city, and we kids each had a music lesson at Ohio State University. Mom, meantime, took the family wash to the laundromat and filled the huge milk cans with drinking water.

After music lessons there was supper at the university cafeteria, and often we went swimming at the gym. In the strange and chlorine-perfumed recesses of the women's locker room, Roo and I, aged four and six, would sneak

shy and wondering looks at grown ladies struggling into girdles or strolling naked and unconcerned to the showers.

When we got home, way past our bedtimes, there would be a pie Mom had made during the day, or buttery, crunchy apple crisp. We poured milk on it, and it was gone too soon.

Apple Crisp
Serves 8

8 cups peeled and thinly sliced tart apples
(such as Granny Smith)
3 teaspoons cinnamon
1 teaspoon salt
½ cup water
1½ cups all-purpose flour
1 cup firmly packed brown sugar
1 cup granulated sugar
¾ cup butter

Preheat the oven to 350 degrees. Grease a 9 by 13-inch pan.

Place the sliced apples in the pan; sprinkle with the cinnamon, salt, and water. Cut together the flour, sugars, and butter until the mixture looks like fine crumbs. Sprinkle the crumbs over the apples. Bake for 45 minutes.

After a few years we moved into town. We kids didn't know how hard it must have been on our parents to live so many miles from the city, especially in the winter. Re-

turning to the farm after those Wednesday excursions, there were many times when the car simply stopped at the bottom of the snowy lane. Mom would pile groceries, clean laundry, water cans, library books, and musical instruments onto sleds for us to pull up the hill. The dog capered about delightedly, trying to pull things off the sleds into the snow.

The worst thing about leaving the farm was giving up Pokey. She would have been miserable in the suburban housing development we were moving to, so with tears and hugs, we gave her to a seeing-eye dogs program. She spent the rest of her days guiding a blind nurse in Cincinnati. We said goodbye to the woods and the old ruined barn, and to the oak trees along the lane. The big empty house was full of echoes.

The farm is gone now—the house, the willows, "suicide hill," all flooded twenty years ago when Alum Creek was dammed. All we have left is the memory of it. In mine, it is always snowing, and four scarved and mittened little girls and their brother are frolicking in the drifts with a laughing German shepherd.

I know what I want for Christmas. I want my childhood back.
> —Robert Fulghum,
> *All I Really Need to Know I
> Learned in Kindergarten*

We still go sledding at Christmas. Karol, who has the toboggan, is the one to roust the rest of us out of the house to play. Holiday coziness is all very well, but one can become quietly deranged after three or four days indoors with what would appear to be a hundred children underfoot. What's more, we've been eating steadily for days, barely moving a muscle. An afternoon in the bright Iowa cold is good for soul and body; the cobwebs clear from your brain, and soon you're raring to eat again. In the meantime, there are snow angels to make, and snow messages to tramp in the neighbors' yards.

"Let's post Mr. Daniel a snowball through his letterbox."
"Let's write things in the snow."
"Let's write, 'Mr. Daniel looks like a spaniel' all over his lawn."
　　　　　　　　　　—Dylan Thomas,
　　　　　　　　　　A Child's Christmas in Wales

Of course there is always the possibility of too much of a good thing. In Iowa it gets *really* cold, and the wind tears around with a vengeance. One year the temperature fell to twenty degrees below zero a few days before Christmas, and stayed there. John and I were driving home from Washington, and someplace in Illinois the car hit an invisible patch of ice. It waltzed gracefully across two lanes of highway and floated into a deep ditch full of snow. I said a tiny prayer of thanks that we were alive, and took a tiny sip of bourbon from a bottle we'd brought to douse the fruitcake. We sat there in the very cold, wondering what next, until a cheerful angel wearing greasy overalls and driving a tow truck pulled up alongside and yanked us out.

We made it home, but the cold persisted and immobilized Ames. Undaunted, the men in the family attempted to gather for their annual "Boys Breakfast." Boys Breakfast had been instigated as an occasion for the guys to get to know each other better, and was generally held at the local Perkins Pancake House. It included Dad, Gary, the brothers-in-law, and more recently, Gary's son, Nathan, and Karol's Jonny. (The excluded sisters have suspicions that Boys Breakfast is a boisterous occasion, with much swapping of sports lore, slapping of backs, and smoking of cigars. John assures me that they simply eat pancakes quietly and enjoy being out of our range.)

In any event, while assembling for Boys Breakfast that Christmas, first one car went off the road and into a ditch, then another. A pickup truck that had been sent to fetch them went in too, then a fourth car simply wouldn't start up at all. In the course of the morning, fully six cars either got stuck in the snow or were stone cold dead from the cold. The guys grimly persevered, however, and they staggered into Perkins to revive themselves with stacks of buttered pancakes and pots of coffee.

A very fine thing about the cold is how wonderful it feels to get out of it. For holiday goodwill,

there's nothing quite like kicking off your snowy boots and hunkering down to purr in front of the fireplace with a mug of mulled wine or hot cocoa.

The mulled wine recipe we particularly like has brandy and fruit in it. When heated, the mixture is lovely and intoxicating, particularly when you drink it while watching the logs on the fire spit and pop and crackle. We make it by combining four cups of water, two cups of sugar, ten whole cloves, and eight cinnamon sticks, and then boiling the mixture for five minutes. Then we add three sliced lemons and let it stand for ten minutes. Last of all, we toss in a third of a cup of brandy and a half gallon of jug red wine and heat it without boiling.

It did not take long to prepare the brew and thrust the tin heater well into the red heart of the fire; and soon every field-mouse was sipping and coughing and choking (for a little mulled ale goes a long way) and wiping his eyes and laughing and forgetting he had ever been cold in all his life.

—Kenneth Grahame,
The Wind in the Willows

Our friend Christie Dailey gave us the recipe for a terrific hot drink that she makes for her large clan every Christmas. They call it hot buttered rum, though it's different than most people's notion of that drink (a jigger of rum, a teaspoon of sugar, boiling water, and a pat of butter floating on top). The Daileys make a mixture of sugar and butter beaten together with eggs. They keep it in the refrigerator

until they want a mugful. Then they stir a big tablespoonful in a mug with a jigger and a half of rum, and fill the mug to the top with boiling water. It's actually more along the lines of what folks used to call a "Tom and Jerry." The quantity this recipe makes says something about how exuberantly the Daileys celebrate Christmas, and how good their brew is.

The Daileys' Hot Buttered Rum

About 35 servings

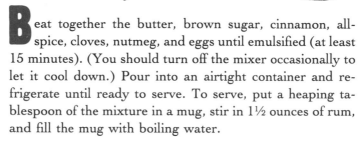

2 cups (1 pound) butter, melted
2 pounds light brown sugar
1 teaspoon cinnamon
1 teaspoon allspice
1 teaspoon ground cloves
1 teaspoon nutmeg
4 eggs
Rum
Boiling water

Beat together the butter, brown sugar, cinnamon, allspice, cloves, nutmeg, and eggs until emulsified (at least 15 minutes). (You should turn off the mixer occasionally to let it cool down.) Pour into an airtight container and refrigerate until ready to serve. To serve, put a heaping tablespoon of the mixture in a mug, stir in 1½ ounces of rum, and fill the mug with boiling water.

The first snow of winter, the first cup of hot cider, the first pumpkin pie, and caramel apples and pot roast—all remind us of those winters when we were children together, stamping our snowy little boots and throwing off our mittens in Mom's kitchen. And now we do what she did. We make soups and stews and homemade bread and apple pies to warm up our families. And on a stormy winter night, we close the drapes and build a fire and draw a little closer to the people we love. Remembering snow.

Tea Party

Like many little girls, we grew up having tea parties. There were outdoor tea parties with acorn cups, leaf plates, and twigs for silverware, and tea parties for dolls and bears in the middle of the living room floor. We had formal teas where we draped ourselves in cast-off scarves, jewelry, skirts, and high heels from our "dress-up box." We had invisible tea with invisible cakes, and real tea (with lots of milk) and bread-and-sugar sandwiches. We're delighted to see that afternoon tea has again become fashionable. What took everybody so long?

For their earliest tea parties, Kath and Karol used a tiny china tea set that had been Mom's when she was a kid. The little teapot fell to the floor during a sisters' brawl and its handle broke off. The girls were paralyzed with horror, but Kathy, with the wisdom of her six years, knew just what to do to keep Mom from finding out about the disaster: She washed the broken piece down the sink. All fixed.

The very first tea party I remember took place when Roo and I were preschoolers, and we were visiting Grandma and Grandpa's Elm Street house in Bluffton, Ohio. There were two little boys who lived next door at the time, and

we hated one another on the spot. The boys bothered us. Grandma, who was the kindest person on earth, tried to end the bad will by inviting the brats over for a tea party. We knew better. Hostilities were suspended only long enough to drink tea and eat jelly sandwiches from the little metal doll dishes Grandma had brought from India. Roo and I weren't very nice. We thought she hadn't noticed.

About thirty years later, Grandma gave us a book of her poems and writings for Christmas. To our chagrin, we found she had written a poem — based on Robert Frost's line about walls: "Before I built a wall, I'd ask to know what I am walling in or walling out." Her poem described the failed tea party as vividly as if it had happened yesterday, and gently chided us for "walling out" the bothersome little boys while pretending to wall them in.

We four sisters had a grown-up afternoon tea together one year in Chicago, when we met for what was to become our first annual sisters' Christmas shopping reunion. Karol, Roo, and I flew to that most Christmassy of cities to meet Kathy, who'd reserved a hotel room for us downtown. She was there first, to decorate the room and stash away the big plate of fudge, bags of caramel corn and peanuts, and a couple of bottles of red wine. They were for later, when we would stay up all night talking.

We dropped our bags at the room, jostled in front of the

lone mirror to fix our makeup and hair, and changed into dress-up clothes. Then we four pranced off to a big fancy dining room for afternoon tea, imagining that everyone knew we were sisters and wished they could be us. A harpist played, a Christmas tree sparkled, the waiter flirted, and the scones and jam and pastries kept coming. All we needed was matching red plaid jumpers.

Afterwards, fueled with sugar and one another's company, we headed into the windy, snowy, glittery cold to goggle at Chicago's thousands of trees covered with twinkling lights and to peer into Marshall Field's Christmas windows.

Later, impressed by the scones at our Chicago tea party, we set out to make them ourselves. We found books of scone recipes, and now we love them all: currant, orange-poppyseed, gingerbread, and date-nut scones. It occurred to me, though, that the fanciest of scone recipes has been in our very own family all along. We know it by the name of "stackup," but the method is the same as that used for a scone. And the buttery, crumbly pastry is just like its elegant English cousin, the classic cream scone. No, not just like. Better.

Stackups are made with biscuit dough, which you roll out thin, brush with melted butter and cinnamon sugar, cut into strips, and then stack about six layers high. (A pastry cloth and a floured sock for your rolling pin are helpful here, because, as is its irksome wont, biscuit dough really sticks to the kitchen counter.) You cut the stacks of buttered and sugared dough into chunks, then you turn each pile of dough on its side and squish it into a muffin tin. When they bake, the biscuit "petals" fluff out, and there you are.

Stackups
Makes 1 dozen

2 cups all-purpose flour
½ teaspoon salt
4 teaspoons baking powder
½ teaspoon cream of tartar
3 tablespoons sugar
½ cup butter or margarine
⅔ cup milk

¼ cup melted butter
½ cup sugar
2 teaspoons cinnamon

Preheat the oven to 375 degrees. Grease a muffin tin.
Mix together the flour, salt, baking powder, cream of tartar, and sugar. Cut in the butter until the mixture resembles fine crumbs. Add the milk, and stir just until the dry particles are moistened. Turn onto a floury board and

give it a few kneads to make the dough hold together. Roll into a big square, about ¼ inch thick. Spread with the melted butter, and sprinkle with the sugar and cinnamon. Cut into long strips about 2 inches wide, and stack the strips on top of one another, about six high. (A pancake turner helps here.) Cut each stack of strips into pieces about 2 inches long, and nestle them into the muffin cups, cut side up. Bake for 15 minutes.

Another year, Karol and Kath and Roo and I met in Washington, D.C., for our Christmas shopping reunion. On the afternoon of the sisters' arrival from the Midwest, the city was hit with the worst winter storm in years — eight inches of snow in an afternoon. I spent a couple of tearful hours racing from terminal to terminal trying to locate their planes, which had been rerouted to New York or were sitting on the ground in Des Moines and Cincinnati.

But in the end all three planes miraculously landed in Washington, and by late afternoon we were drinking tea in front of the fire in my living room. The snow piled softly outside, and it was so quiet that it seemed as if every boot and wheel on Capitol Hill had been mittened. There were homemade scones, of course, and chocolate shortbread hearts with red sugar sprinkled on them. After tea, fearless shoppers to the core, we floundered through the drifts to the subway and headed towards the department stores—open, and magically

deserted—for a quick two hours of Christmas shopping before they closed for the night.

Grandma used to make sweet milky Indian tea, called *chai,* for Kathy and Karol's tea parties on the front porch when they visited her as little girls. They draped themselves in Indian cotton saris, and she taught them how to make marigold necklaces, just the way the Indian women in her village did.

Shortly before Grandma died, when she was very frail and a little uncertain, Kathy and her husband, Jim, and I visited her at the Mennonite nursing home in Goshen, Indiana. Her dear friend Thelma Groff, who had also been a missionary in India, seemed to know how much Grandma missed being able to do things for us. So Thelma planned something very lovely. She invited us all to an Indian meal and afterwards she took Grandma out to the kitchen for the surprise.

There, with infinite patience, she and Grandma made *chai.* They simmered two cinnamon sticks, eight cardamom pods, and four cloves in five cups of water for about ten minutes, then added a cup of milk and a half cup of sugar and brought it to a simmer again. Then they added five teaspoons of loose black tea leaves, turned off the heat, and let the mixture sit for a couple minutes. Then they strained the *chai* into china cups and served us tea: made with cardamom and love.

Unless you are serving *chai* (which is a lovely, fragrant, comforting indulgence all by itself) the real purpose of a tea party is to eat. Eight of Kathy's friends came to a winter tea party once, all elegant and ladylike. If they weren't *wearing* white gloves and hats with veils, they acted like they were. Nine little fingers curled daintily around nine china tea cups. And then they fell to the food: jam tarts, chocolate tea bread, sausage rolls, shortbread, tea sandwiches, scones, and cookies. A grownup tea party is, quite simply, a wonderful excuse for dressing up, using your pretty china, acting proper, and stuffing yourself.

We think that Mom's china teacup collection probably started this whole tea party thing. Over the past fifty years, Mom has collected an enormous array of beautiful bone china cups and saucers, all colors and shapes. Each piece of china was a gift from Dad or one of us, and every time she takes a cup down from the cupboard she remembers who gave it to her and marvels at how pretty it still is.

Some enchantment protects those cups from harm. Astonishingly, in a household where kids and grandkids have been recklessly washing and drying dishes for decades, and generations of glasses, silverware, and china have crashed to the floor, only a couple of Mom's special cups have been broken. Two loud Siamese cats naughtily walking about on the counter after Sunday dinner broke the spell that time.

Decorating

Now, the tree is decorated with bright merriment, and song, and dance, and cheerfulness. And they are welcome. Innocent and welcome be they ever, held beneath the branches of the Christmas Tree, which cast no gloomy shadow!

—Charles Dickens,
"Impressionistic Sketches"
in *Selected Short Fiction*

It seems that we four sisters start celebrating Christmas earlier every year, what with our November fruitcake baking, our Christmas shopping reunion in early December, and our year-round sewing and embroidering. But Christmas trees are another matter. There should be some kind of cosmic ordinance against putting up Christmas trees until after Thanksgiving. And the same goes for Christmas carols. Thanksgiving is Thanksgiving. People should be eating turkey and appreciating the fact that they're not Pilgrims. Christmas is Christmas. *Now* it's time for the Christmas tree and "Hark the Herald"!

When we were little, putting up the tree signaled the official start to Christmas. We would go out to capture a

Christmas tree in mid-December, and it would lie, trussed and sleeping, on the back porch. About a week before Christmas, the magic day arrived, and Dad would go out and wake it up and bring it into the living room. We waited anxiously while he wrestled the piney giant into its stand, and slowly, slowly, stood it upright.

And then we set about bringing the great, fragrant, beautiful green thing back to life. Dad strung the colored lights in the scratchy branches while Mom opened box after box of ornaments, lifting each one out like an old friend. When Roo and I were preschoolers, we used to pick favorites that we called our own. Hers was a royal-blue sphere with a glitter snowflake on it, and mine a lipstick-pink one with swirls. I think we named and talked to them.

We didn't have very many Christmas things in those days, but they were all so dear to us. We had a cluster of real sleigh bells from a horse's collar for the front door, and a knobby red glass bowl on a pedestal with tiny candles to float in it, given by our favorite babysitter, Mary. There was a row of little china bells on the mantelpiece, one for each of us. Best of all was a Frosty the Snowman lamp. He sat on an end table, smiling fatly in his little black top hat. Frosty must have burned out and been thrown away about thirty years ago. We would give anything to have him now.

Everyone's favorite ornaments for a time, until we lost them, were Roo's "glow angels." The glow angels were a flock of tiny pale-green luminescent plastic angels, hanging in a sort of mid-flight crouch from their hooks. When you turned off all the lights (or went into a closet with one cupped in your hand and closed the door behind you), they did indeed glow. Roo was so enchanted with the glow angels that she took them from the tree and trotted back and forth to the closet to work the miracle again and again. In the course of just a few Christmases, they were gone. But somewhere, in the back of a very dark closet in Ohio, there is an entire choir of little plastic Christmas tree angels. And they're glowing.

The glow angels make me think of the marvelous Christmas tree a friend of mine puts up every year. Instead of ornaments, she decorates it with favorite treasures saved over a lifetime. There's Fog's cat collar, kept to remember her by, hanging from one branch on a gold cord. And purple plastic Mardi Gras beads from dinner at a Cajun restaurant, glass animals from a childhood collection, costume jewelry, matchbooks and boxes from special places, a feather from the Des Moines zoo, little stuffed animals, toys and gadgets, a Japanese parasol and fan, and the key and key chain from a long-gone Karmann Ghia.

O Christmas tree, O Christmas tree,
thy leaves are so unchanging.
O Christmas tree, O Christmas tree,
thy leaves are so unchanging.
Not only green when summer's here,
but also when 'tis cold and drear.
O Christmas tree, O Christmas tree,
thy leaves are so unchanging.

—Traditional carol

Well, I don't know about "unchanging." Karol and Jonny once had a tree that changed pretty dramatically. They bought it and set it up in their living room just a few weeks before Christmas. They covered it with ornaments and little wrapped packages, and very proud they were, too. In short order, however, the tree proceeded to lose its needles—extravagantly. Every time someone walked through the living room, the vibrations brought down showers of needles.

By Christmas Eve there really weren't any needles on the tree at all, and the branches drooped down in complete defeat. Every couple of minutes, an ornament would slide down a limp, naked bough, crash to the floor, and break. It was an absurd Dr. Seuss Christmas tree, and we all fell about laughing every time we came into Karol and Jonny's house.

34

Karol was embarrassed and wanted to take it down before Christmas, but Jonathan, quite properly, would hear of no such thing. It was a question of solidarity.

Once a year, Christmas decorations transform your house and your ordinary world — and you — into something funny and special and magic. Think about it: when else do sober and respectable citizens put reindeer on their front lawns? But the doing of it is even more important than the effect. And that's why we like to make things.

When Kath and Karol were very little, Dad organized a paper chain factory in the dining room. He found bright, stiff, shiny paper, and cut out hundreds of red and green strips. The little girls carefully stapled them closed, and together they produced a chain that snaked through the living room, hall, and kitchen. Certainly the immense paper chain looked marvelous — we kept it for years. But what Kathy and Karol remember best was the rare pleasure of having Dad all to themselves while they made decorations for Christmas.

All four of us make things for our own and each other's houses at Christmas. Roo has a green and white table runner that I covered with cross-stitched Christmas trees. Karol hangs up a lumpy stuffed wreath that I made for her kitchen years ago, and Roo's handmade ceramic stars grace all our Christmas trees. Kathy embroidered each of us a little ornament with our initials on it, and so on.

It was probably kindergarten that started us down the road to making Christmas decorations. Kathy got hopelessly hooked first, when as a five-year-old she covered a hedge apple with gold paint and brought it home to Mother as a Christmas decoration. Lots has changed since those days, but for spreading around Christmas cheer, it's hard to beat a can of gold spray paint. The very sight of one gives us more Christmassy shivers than the Hallelujah Chorus. We collect pinecones (and Roo picks up those little spiky gum-tree balls) all year round, spray them gold, and put them everywhere at Christmas. Last year Kath lost all control and sprayed her stash of pinecones in the backyard in July.

And there are those Styrofoam balls stuck all over with toothpicks, piled into a Christmas tree shape, and flocked with spray snow. Every home needs one at Christmas. Karol made a beauty when she was a kid, but it was a fleeting thing: the Styrofoam was inferior and fell apart under the assault of the toothpicks. She's made toothpick Christmas trees since with more muscular Styrofoam, and with round, instead of flat, toothpicks, which had shredded the foam. (The same technique is a natural for stars and planets, just in case there's a grade-school science fair coming up.)

When we were kids we were able to get little wooden spheres, about the size of a cherry, with faces painted on them. For some reason, Swan Cleaners in Columbus, Ohio, gave them away when you picked up your laundry. Many of our Christmas decorating projects, such as the famous shoebox crèche, required them. We'd nag Mom to drive us into town in search of Swan Cleaners heads, whether or not we had dry cleaning to leave. We thought of the cleaners as first and foremost the place to get those heads, and never quite understood that the quid pro quo was paying them to do one's laundry.

The holiday crafts I like the best are the ones involving those marvelous crisp, gaudy Christmas cottons. Come October, fabric stores stock tables full of Christmas fabric. There are stars, poinsettias, candy canes, and snowmen by the yard. Sometimes the fabric even has glitter on it — oh joy! A couple of years ago, I came under the spell of a bolt of holly-sprinkled cotton. It was so beautiful that I wanted to cover my entire house and body with the stuff. I sprinted to the cash register and bought about twenty yards. All the way home on the subway I sneaked looks at it, my mouth watering furiously.

Once I had reluctantly conceded that I could not wear holly-printed cotton to the office, I set about making a few things (oh, all right, hundreds of things) out of it. The best were the slip-on covers for the toss pillows on my living room sofa. The neat thing about these covers is that they go on and off effortlessly, in the event that Christmas-printed cotton should ever pall.

Here's how it's done. To cover an eighteen-inch pillow, cut one nineteen-inch square of fabric and set it aside. Also cut two rectangles of fabric, nineteen inches by twelve inches. Machine-hem one long side of each of the rectangles. (To machine-hem, turn the raw edge under to the wrong side about a quarter of an inch, and press. Turn it to the wrong side again, and press. Stitch the twice-folded edge. Nice and refined.)

Now take one of your hemmed rectangle pieces and place it on top of the nineteen-inch square, right sides together and matching the raw edges. Pin the edges. Next take the other hemmed rectangle and place it on the other end of the square, right sides together and matching the edges. It will overlap the other rectangle. (Don't scream at it; it's supposed to.) Pin it, and then sew all around the square with a ⅝-inch seam allowance. Trim the seams, then turn the cover right side out and press it.

There now, see what you've done? The overlap lets you push a pillow in and out without zipping, cursing, or tearing. Our next lesson will be the holly cotton tuxedo.

We like our houses so much at Christmas that we were tempted to describe each in loving detail here. But the reason we love our houses at Christmas is, well, because they *are* our houses at Christmas! And the same goes for you. You don't want to hear about Kathy's three Christmas

trees, Roo's white china rabbit ornament, or Karol's wicker basket full of dried flowers and tiny Christmas lights. You have your own tree, all covered with memories and traditions, and your own houseful of beloved old relics. Maybe you even have a Nativity scene with a Swan Cleaners Holy Family.

That said, however, we have a few ideas we'd like to share. We'll call them the Four Midwestern Sisters' Essential Christmas Decorating Tips.

First: Never, never, never throw out a beloved Christmas relic, no matter how shabby it has become. Remember Frosty the Snowman.

Second: Homes are for people, not interior decorators. Make your own decorations, even if it's nothing more complicated than a paper chain or a Christmas card collage.

Third: When you really love a piece of Christmas fabric, there can never be too much. Buy the bolt.

Fourth: Never pass up a pinecone. No matter where you are or what you're doing, pick it up. Take it home. Spray it gold. If you really cannot find room for one more, fill a basket with pinecones and give it to a friend.

Fifth: Deck the halls with boughs of holly. Fa la la la la, la la la la.

Galas

. . . .

We four sisters grew up cooking together, learning how from one another and from our mother. Mom started teaching junior high school English when Roo began the first grade, and from then on we all helped with meals. The pairs of sisters (Kathy and Karol first, then Roo and I) were entrusted to plan, cook, and clean up at least one family meal every week.

We girls made "Jonnie Marzetti" (spaghetti sauce mixed with elbow macaroni) and tucked cottage cheese into canned pear halves to display on an iceberg lettuce leaf. Kathy's favorite offering was a casserole of layered tuna fish, onions, and boiled potatoes, slathered with white sauce and sprinkled with parsley, and Karol's first dessert was coffee ice cream floats.

In those days, family dinner always had a main dish, a vegetable, a salad, and dessert. And everybody was there. Always. At 5:30 p.m. sharp, Mom and Dad were at the head and foot of the table and we had better be in our places too. The food was sturdy, cheap 1950s fare: casseroles, liver and onions, Jell-O mold, and prune whip.

41

We tried out recipes from seventh-grade home economics class, like the adorable "pigs-in-blankets" (biscuit-wrapped wieners), and had knowing conversations about the importance of color and texture on the dinner plate. I loved home-ec class until we came to the "charm and beauty" unit, which was the time for our middle-aged teacher to go around the room and publicly point out each of our twelve-year-old deficiencies. I don't remember what was said about anybody else, but I was benignly informed that I was a little pudgy.

With the exception of the charm and beauty business, though, we four went at home economics with a vengeance, sewing our little dirndl skirts and aprons and making messes in the kitchen. The family cheerfully ate everything we put in front of them. With Mom's encouragement we expanded our repertoire—and fell in love with feeding people.

The first dinner party we kids ever gave was a surprise party for Mom. Dad invited several other couples, and we made dinner. We were very young and none of us was much of a hand at frying chicken, so we bought a bunch from Colonel Sanders's franchise. Kentucky Fried Chicken was new to us, and we thought it was mighty fine. We stealthily disposed of the incriminating cartons and arranged the greasy treasures on a platter, spruced up with parsley. We made everything else ourselves, but the hit of the meal was the chicken. The awful truth emerged when Juanita Harrison requested the recipe.

Until we left Ohio in 1966, our folks didn't entertain

much. But when Dad was appointed head of the Iowa State University music department and we moved to Ames, we were propelled willy-nilly into entertaining on a large scale. Ames has a lively music scene, with regular performances by the local faculty and frequent visits by major symphony orchestras and solo performers. And that meant cocktail parties. And fancy dinners. And hors d'oeuvres. Mom was quite terrified. Good thing she had us girls, aged eleven to nineteen and all living at home, to learn how to do it with her!

Probably the scariest party was the first, a large buffet dinner for the entire music faculty to come and look us over. Needless to say, there wasn't a piece of Kentucky Fried Chicken on the premises. There was a big tossed salad, though, and Chicken Newburg in dear little patty shells with almonds sprinkled on top, which we thought was madly elegant.

Most of our parties consisted of cocktails and snacks after university faculty recitals. We proudly called these soirées "galas," and we had dozens of them over the years. There was always an element of hysteria about our galas because we invariably attended the concert beforehand. In order to get food on the table and the makeup scrubbed off the bathroom counter before the first famished musician rang the doorbell, we had to streak hell-for-leather out of the concert hall before the last clap had died away. It was an awful lot of fun.

We collected recipes, tried out new things, and ate the

failures in the kitchen after everybody left. Ultimately we developed a stable of faithful standbys that we came to think of as our party signatures. Take "Large Orange" punch. We served it at our first party, and ever after. I think it might have been the first alcoholic punch Mom ever tasted, probably at some Ohio State faculty gathering. Delighted with its bourbony orangeness, Mom claimed it as our own and introduced "Large Orange" to Ames. The formula was simple and lethal: whatever quantity one made, two thirds of it was orange juice and one third straight bourbon. We mixed it together in a big bowl, and added an ice ring made with ginger ale and artificial flowers.

We're still using recipes from our post-recital galas. One of the regulars is Cranberry Cocktail Meatballs. They're easy and spicy and festive, in their dark red cranberry sauce, and perfect for the holidays. We serve them in a chafing dish, and people stand there next to it, toothpicks in hand, until they are all gone.

Cranberry Cocktail Meatballs

Makes 2 dozen cocktail-size meatballs

Meatballs
2 pounds ground beef round
1 cup packaged cornflake crumbs
½ cup minced fresh parsley

2 eggs
2 tablespoons soy sauce
1/2 teaspoon freshly ground pepper
1 teaspoon minced garlic
1/3 cup catsup
1/2 cup finely chopped onion

Sauce
1 can (16 ounces) jellied cranberry sauce
1 bottle (12 ounces) chile sauce
1 tablespoon brown sugar
1 tablespoon lemon juice

Mix meatball ingredients together in a large bowl. Form into walnut-size balls, and place in a large square baking dish.

Preheat the oven to 350 degrees. In a saucepan, mix together the sauce ingredients. Stir and simmer until the cranberry sauce melts. Pour over the meatballs and bake, uncovered, for 30 minutes. Serve in a chafing dish.

Because we learned to feed a crowd while we were teenagers, it has never since seemed hard to throw big parties. But why is it that the ones we remember most fondly are the disasters, the screwups, the complete train wrecks? Consider Roo's wedding reception.

Roo and Larry got married in Ames in 1979, on a very hot September day. An important part of this story is that Roo is, well, elegant. She wore a cream-colored wedding dress that Kath had made for her. It was severely cut, like a beautifully tailored silk shirt, and wide-belted at the waist.

And she had pheasant feathers in her bouquet and her hair, and stockings with seams up the back.

In keeping with all this glamour, Roo suggested that we have not a wedding cake but a pastry cart. Since the reception was to be at the house, Karol and I gravely picked up the gauntlet, accepted the challenge, and pledged to produce a pastry cart. The cart part of it was easy; Mom already had a handmade wooden trolley parked in the dining room. The pastries were up to us.

We went at the task with a will (and some help from our grandmother), and by the hour of Roo's wedding there were trays of dessert crêpes, cream puffs, meringues, éclairs, and petits fours sitting neatly in Karol's refrigerator. And Grandma had laboriously cut out dozens of watermelon hearts, using a cookie cutter. They too waited quietly in the refrigerator, just next to the freezer compartment. The last thing we did was to squirt handsome dollops of fake whipped cream from a can all over our creations. Karol and I then sped off to the wedding, joining Kathy and Gary's wife, Marsha, to stand up with Roo while she married Larry.

After the wedding, Karol and I returned to her house to pick up the riches for the pastry cart. To our horror, the trays were swimming in liquid! The cunning little treasures were limp and sodden! The fake whipped cream had collapsed and wet all over our darling cream puffs!

And that wasn't all. Perversely, the refrigerator that

couldn't keep whipped cream chilled had had no problem whatsoever freezing Grandma's pretty watermelon hearts solid. When they thawed, they turned into watermelon Kleenex.

Well, of course there was a happy ending. I flew to the grocery store for some real cream while Karol fell to scrubbing each damp crêpe and éclair with paper towels. We had to chuck Grandma's watermelon hearts, but we mopped up the trays, rearranged our crêpes and cream puffs and meringues, and camouflaged the damage with newly whipped cream. And I think Roo was so happy she never even knew.

Undaunted by the pastry cart experience, Karol has continued to entertain with style. She is the undisputed expert at feeding multitudes and at improvising festivities out of thin air. At a family Christmas brunch last year, for example, Karol served up puff pastry shells stuffed with egg salad, and an enormous pan of pecan sticky buns. There was fizzy red punch, and hot chocolate with a candy cane stuck in it and whipped cream on top. Karol used a colored sheet for a tablecloth, tied the napkins in plaid ribbons, and put a candle at every place. Aside from the fact that her terrier, Jackie, leaped five feet straight up into the air and snatched a tray of egg puffs off the counter, it was a perfect occasion.

More than any of us, Karol makes up recipes. The products are always great, but like most improvisers, she's irritatingly negligent about writing down precise quantities.

In a discussion of her famous mincemeat trifle, for example, all I could winkle out of her were hazy references to "splashes of rum" and "a bunch of Mom's mincemeat." We pinned her down on her stuffed mushrooms, though, and stood at her side with a notebook while she sautéed the pepperoni filling and popped them in the oven.

Stuffed Mushrooms

Makes 20 hors d'oeuvres

> *20 large mushrooms*
> *3½ ounces packaged pepperoni, finely chopped*
> *¼ cup finely chopped onions*
> *¼ cup bread crumbs*
> *5 tablespoons spaghetti sauce*
> *¼ teaspoon Tabasco sauce*
> *1 tablespoon Parmesan cheese*

Preheat the oven to 350 degrees.
Wash the mushrooms and pat dry. Cut off the stems and reserve the caps. Mince the mushroom stems. Sauté the pepperoni and onion along with the minced mushroom stems until onions are soft, about 7 minutes. Drain excess fat from the pan. Stir the bread crumbs into the pepperoni mixture, along with spaghetti sauce, Tabasco sauce, and Parmesan cheese. Stuff the mushroom caps, and bake for 15 minutes, or until done.

I think what I miss most at my galas in Washington is the fun of having sisters around to laugh and cook with. But we do send recipes over the fax machine or in the mail, and spend hours on the phone comparing menus and swapping gala horror stories. And on occasion we fly across the country to attend each other's Christmas parties. This year, for example, Karol and Jonny flew to Washington to help John and me with our caroling party. And I began my own holiday gala tradition after flying out to Illinois for Kathy's. It was one heck of a party.

Kathy's idea of a very good time is to spend weeks making beautiful, scrumptious little hors d'oeuvres and snacks and squirreling them into the freezer. Then a couple days before the party, she knocks off work, and marshaling her kitchen tools, groceries, husband, and daughter like a general before a battle, she moves into her Christmas Cooking Frenzy mode. She churns out snack after snack, filling two refrigerators and a freezer. The day of the party, she puts additional trays out to cool in the garage, on the roof of the car.

Now this isn't going to sound like fun to normal people, but here's what happens during the party itself. Kath spends the entire time in the kitchen, whisking things in and out of the oven, the microwave, and the deep-fryer. Every appliance in the kitchen goes at full blast, and a throng of friends wait expectantly in the dining room for each new plate of appetizers to emerge, hot and crisp and wonderful.

The first time Kath ever gave this Christmas party was

in Storm Lake, Iowa, where Jim was teaching at a small liberal arts college. On that occasion, a large, loud woman planted herself solidly by the dining room table. As Kathy brought out each new appetizer, this guest, designating herself as the official taster and herald, sampled one, then trumpeted forth, "Now this one's a cheese puff" or "Here come the salami pinwheels." She would then regale the crowd with a critique of the treat, and wait for the next.

Kath continues to send forth her party food into an admiring crowd, albeit without a one-woman Greek chorus. And the wonder of it is that she manages to pull it off every year, sane and happy, without ruining her plaid taffeta Christmas skirt!

We think that none of this would be possible without the years of training in kitchen chaos with Mom and the sisters at our house in Ames. But it's certainly also true that the Lockards' Christmas gala wouldn't happen without Katie to take coats and hand around plates of snacks and Jim to welcome guests and serve the hot cider.

Jim's cider routine is a nice one, festive and easy. He heats the cider in a huge coffee urn with handfuls of cinnamon sticks and cloves in the filter basket. (That way they don't clog up the spigot.) Next to the urn stands a decanter of Kentucky bourbon, and guests spike—or don't spike—their Christmas cider as they like. "Large Apple," served hot! At the end of the evening they substitute hot coffee for cider, and pass around a big plate of fudge.

The best Christmas fudge in the business is our Mom's. She used to make it in tiny batches, beating it on an old china plate until the sugar dissolved completely, and then turning it out on the counter to knead like bread until it was melty and creamy. The beating and kneading took forever, and Mom used to boast that she got her strong right arm from milking cows on the farm when she was a girl.

I made it this year, following Mom's instructions assiduously. I melted the butter, and added in dribs and drabs of cream and sugar. I cooked it (without stirring, just like she said) until it got to the "soft ball" stage. Then I came to the part where you are supposed to pour the molten mass onto a buttered plate and beat it with a wooden spoon. I gave it a few jabs with the spoon. It resisted. I tried again. Beat, beat. By then I was utterly exhausted. I gave it another three beats and gave up. Mom used to beat and knead it for what seemed like hours, and I was defeated after ten seconds. What's more, my fudge had an unpleasant unfudgy appearance. Dirt, actually, is what it rather resembled.

In a dudgeon, I scraped the mess off the plate, threw it into my food processor, and whirled it around for a few minutes. To my great wonder, it transformed itself into silky smooth fudge. I tried a piece or three. It tasted great! Here's the recipe, then, with a little more chocolate than Mom used

in the tan-colored, delicately flavored original. But don't try it if you don't have a food processor, because it's pretty clear that we can't keep up with our moms without a lot of fancy kitchen machinery. But then, we never developed a strong right arm milking cows on the farm.

Velvety Kneaded Fudge

Makes approximately 2½ dozen pieces

2 tablespoons butter
3 tablespoons Dutch-process unsweetened cocoa
2 cups sugar
10 tablespoons half-and-half
Dash of salt
1 teaspoon vanilla extract

Melt the butter in a saucepan over low heat. Stir in the cocoa. Add the sugar, alternating with the half-and-half. Add the salt. Stir until the sugar is dissolved. Cook over low heat—*do not stir*—until a candy thermometer registers the soft ball stage (240 degrees). Remove from the heat and cool at room temperature for about 20 minutes.

Pour the candy mixture and vanilla into a food processor and process, stopping frequently to scrape the sides of the bowl for about 5 minutes, or until thick, smooth, and satiny. Working quickly to prevent drying, roll into two logs about 1 inch in diameter, and wrap each tightly in plastic wrap. When ready to serve, cut the rolls into chunks.

My Washington, D.C., Christmas gala has none of the Cecil B. DeMille quality of Kathy's. Since I'm neither calm enough nor neat enough to pull off the feat of deep-fat-frying appetizers in my good clothes, I make almost all my snacks ahead of time, then set them out on the table and let the chips fall where they may. There are cheese balls and squares of cold artichoke quiche, smoked turkey–blue cheese pinwheels and salmon dip, platters of cookies and baskets of shortbread. And they're all made in advance.

I think the appetizer my guests like the best is my husband's hummus. John's mother's side of the family is Syrian-American, and he grew up eating hummus and other Middle Eastern foods. John's mom, Nell, whose parents came to the United States from Damascus in the early 1900s, tells me that her mother left all the garlic out of the ethnic dishes she made for their family, for fear that the kids would be teased for eating "immigrant's food." We are happy to leave the garlic in, and serve bowls of hummus alongside wooden platters of pita bread cut into triangles and toasted. There's never a drop left at the end of our Christmas gala.

John's Hummus

Makes 3½ cups

2 cans (18 ounces) garbanzo beans, drained,
*   liquid reserved*
Juice and grated peel of 1 lemon
4 tablespoons tahini (sesame paste)
2-4 teaspoons crushed garlic, to taste
½ teaspoon salt
2 tablespoons reserved garbanzo bean liquid
4 tablespoons water

Place all ingredients in a blender or food processor, and blend until perfectly smooth. Refrigerate, covered, for at least 24 hours for flavor to ripen. Serve with toasted pita triangles or melba toast.

In my view, a Christmas gala isn't a Christmas gala without fruitcake. Fruitcake gets a bum rap, what with all those mean jokes about there being only a dozen or so extant fruitcakes, which keep being recycled until everybody in America gets one of the twelve. It is my firmly held conviction that if fruitcake didn't have to compete with Mom's peanut brittle, people would eat a lot more of it!

In addition to the fact that I happen to love fruitcake, I bake them every year because it gives me the excuse to start celebrating Christmas early. On a Sunday afternoon right after Thanksgiving, I round up my fruitcake pans and buy a mess of dried fruit. And while the fruitcakes bake, I

sit on my high stool in the kitchen, leafing through cook-
books and dreaming of Christmas.

*It's always the same: a morning arrives in November, and my
friend, as though officially inaugurating the Christmas time of
year that exhilarates her imagination and fuels the blaze of her
heart, announces: "It's fruitcake weather!"*

— Truman Capote, *A Christmas Memory*

I have tried lots of fruitcake recipes over the years, including a chocolate one, which I burned, and a Kentucky
fruitcake whose principal — maybe only — ingredients were
cherries, nuts, and bourbon. But my favorite, by far, was
given to me by my dear pal Ann (Betsy) Peterson. She and
I were friends in high school in Ames, and happily we both
ended up in Washington. She pitches in and sings tenor at
my Christmas caroling gala, I play the piano at hers, and
apricot fruitcake is found at both.

Ann's and my fruitcake is lighter than most, apricot-
studded and flavored with orange liqueur. Ann's recipe
includes a pound each of apricots, raisins, candied cherries,
and dates, but for mine I double the apricots and raisins
and leave out the rest of the fruit. This year I substituted
a pound of dried sour cherries for half the apricots, and it
was sensational.

Apricot fruitcake is so wonderful that I make the full
recipe. There's so much dried fruit that I have to mix it up

in a dishpan, but it's worth the trouble. However, if you don't want to make four loaves, the recipe is easily halved.

Apricot Fruitcake
Makes 4 loaves

2 pounds dried apricots, chopped
2 pounds golden raisins
1 pound almonds, blanched, toasted, and chopped
1 pound pecans, chopped
4 cups all-purpose flour
2 cups (1 pound) butter, softened
1½ cups brown sugar
1½ cups granulated sugar
12 eggs
1 teaspoon ground cloves
2 teaspoons cinnamon
1 teaspoon mace
1½ teaspoons baking soda
1 teaspoon salt
¼ cup rum
¼ cup orange liqueur
¼ cup brandy
Juice and peel of two oranges
Juice and peel of two lemons

Preheat the oven to 300 degrees. Thoroughly grease and flour four 8 by 5 by 3-inch pans. Dredge the dried fruit and nuts with 1 cup of the flour.

Cream together the butter and sugars. Add the eggs, one at a time, beating after each addition. Sift the remaining flour with the spices, baking soda, and salt, and add to the creamed mixture alternating with the rum, liqueur, brandy, and fruit juices. Stir in the orange and lemon peel. Pour the batter over the dried fruit and stir until well blended.

Pour the batter into the prepared loaf pans. Set the pans in a large roasting pan and pour 1 to 2 inches of hot water into the roasting pan. Bake for 2½ to 3 hours, until the cakes pull away from the edges of the pans and a cake tester comes out clean. Cool on wire racks for 10 minutes, then remove cakes from pans.

When completely cool, wrap the cakes in cheesecloth dampened with brandy or orange liqueur, and store in a covered container.

These fruitcakes will keep for at least three months, if well wrapped. They should be refrigerated for several hours before attempting to slice them, as they will otherwise crumble.

After I moved away from Ames, the Christmas treat I missed the most was Mom's peanut brittle. I never made peanut brittle at home because she always did. My job was to eat it. Being apart from your family in the weeks before Christmas was bad enough, but to bear it without peanut brittle was insupportable. So shortly before my very first Washington Christmas party, I rang her on the phone to get her recipe. It seemed straightforward enough, but apparently raw peanuts are too exotic a delicacy

to be found on the East Coast. I scoured Washington and environs for raw peanuts. There wasn't one to be found, not in health food stores, supermarkets, or specialty shops. In desperation I phoned home again, and three days later a large box of Mom's peanut brittle arrived, just in time for my party.

Burkhalter Peanut Brittle

Makes 2 pounds brittle

2 cups sugar
1 cup water
1 cup light corn syrup
2 teaspoons butter
1 pound shelled raw peanuts
2 teaspoons baking soda
1 teaspoon vanilla extract

Lightly butter a cookie sheet.
Combine the sugar, water, and corn syrup in a heavy saucepan. Cook, stirring, over low heat until sugar dissolves. Bring to a boil. Boil gently *without stirring* until it reaches 228 degrees on a candy thermometer. (Brush down the sugar crystals as they form on the pan.)
Add the butter and peanuts. Boil, stirring, until the mixture reaches 306 degrees on the candy thermometer. (It will seem as if it's taking forever for the mixture to reach hard-crack stage, but when it does it happens fast. Watch closely so the peanuts don't burn at the end.)

Remove from the heat, and stir in the baking soda and vanilla. (The baking soda will make the candy froth up. Don't worry.) Pour onto the prepared cookie sheet, working quickly because it's going to get hard fast. Spread out as thin as possible. Let harden, and break into pieces.

Between Mom and the four of us sisters, this business of phoning up for a recipe occurs about every five minutes as Christmas approaches. Once Kathy phoned me for some last-minute kibitzing just before my holiday gala. As we talked, I spooned the filling for a fancy "goat cheesecake" appetizer into its crushed-cracker crust.

Impressed, she demanded the recipe on the spot. I reeled off the ingredients: goat cheese, cream cheese, eggs, pepper, dill, flour. Flour. What flour? Oh, woe! I've got guests coming in an hour, and I forgot the flour. The omission would have meant goat cheese soup swimming in a cracker crust, and the phone line rang with shrieks. With the phone still tucked under my ear and Kathy cheering me on, I attempted to undo the damage. The result was a rather goaty-looking cheesecake, with cracker crumbs swirled throughout the filling and bald patches in the crust. But we ate it.

Christmas Cookies

More than any other holiday food, Christmas cookies hurtle you straight back to your childhood. Everything else may have changed, but Christmas cookies still taste exactly the way they did when you were five.

We always had hundreds of Christmas cookies around our place during the holidays. I'm not sure why, then, it was necessary for us kids to hoard them one Christmas a long time ago.

It was around 1959, when Kathy and Karol were twelve and nine years old. They thought it would be bold and fine for us kids to get up in the middle of the night on Christmas Eve and eat cookies. For days we furtively grabbed an extra handful when the plate made its way around the table after dinner, and squirreled them away in our pockets and closets. We had a heavy old dining room table with a peculiar feature that seemed designed to facilitate cookie hoarding: a little recessed shelf about two inches deep, which ran all the way around the table. It was also very useful for stashing undesirable green vegetables or hideous partially chewed chunks of some hated food, such as liver.

With the aid of the subversive table and numerous hit-and-run raids on the kitchen between meals, we managed to collect a large cache of Christmas cookies. Mom and Dad probably knew and probably didn't care, but it was important that we five thought it was daring, and very wrong.

At 2:00 a.m. on Christmas morning, Kathy and Karol's alarm clock went off. They tried to lure us from our beds to join them in a cookie party, but we little ones were too warmly tucked in to join them in rebellion in the middle of a dark and silent house. So in the end the big sisters ate our cookie hoard — by now linty, stale, and crumbly — and waited with great impatience for Christmas.

We happen to think that cookies are the staff of life, all year round. But at Christmas they are much, much more. Their once-a-year specialness is what sets the holiday apart and reminds you of Mom, and Grandma, and all the cookie bakers who have loved you. They turn the kitchen into the center of the universe and pull us in like a magnet.

And another thing. They taste better than anything on earth.

There are three rules about Christmas cookies, and they

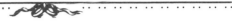

should be committed to memory, right here and now. First, Christmas cookies should be served only at Christmas. It is a crime against nature to serve a springerle any time but December. (Well, *maybe*, if there are any left, during the first few weeks of January—but we're warning you, it could confuse things and produce an extra month of winter.)

Springerle, by the way, are pure white, anise-flavored, rock-hard squares with a pretty imprint on their tops. The little decoration comes from a sort of quilted rolling pin. Mom shapes the dough with her fingers into a square exactly the width of the rolling pin and at least an inch thick. Then she gives it one firm, hard roll with the springerle rolling pin, pressing down hard, which flattens the dough to about half an inch. Next she cuts around the impressions with a knife and lifts them onto the cookie sheet, which is covered with crushed anise seeds. If you don't own a magic springerle rolling pin, you are allowed to cut out the dough with ordinary cutters, but make sure it's nice and thick: about half an inch.

The preferred way to eat a springerle is to dunk it daintily into a cup of coffee, then quickly stuff the whole thing into your mouth before the soggy part breaks off and slops onto the tablecloth. Repeat ten times.

Springerle

Makes about 3 dozen

4 eggs
2 cups sugar
½ teaspoon anise extract
¼ teaspoon vanilla extract
1 teaspoon grated lemon peel
4 cups all-purpose flour
½ teaspoon baking soda
¼ teaspoon salt
¼ cup crushed anise seeds

Beat the eggs until thick, about 5 minutes, with an electric mixer. Add the sugar gradually, beating well. Continue beating for 5 minutes. Blend in the anise and vanilla extracts, and lemon peel. Mix the flour with the baking powder and salt, and blend that into the egg mixture completely. Wrap dough in plastic wrap and chill for several hours or overnight.

Lightly grease two cookie sheets, and sprinkle with the anise seeds. Pat the dough out with your hands, about an inch thick. Roll across it just once with a special springerle rolling pin. Cut the squares out along the imprints, and place on the prepared cookie sheets. Cover with a cloth, and let stand 8 hours or overnight on the counter.

Preheat the oven to 375 degrees. Place the cookies in the oven and immediately reduce the heat to 300 degrees. Bake for 10 minutes. *Do not brown.*

Let cookies stand, tightly covered, in an airtight container for at least 2 weeks to mellow.

The second rule about Christmas cookies is that they are full of butter and low on vitamins and there should be absolutely no bemoaning that fact. Christmas cookies nourish those brain cells that produce comfort and happiness, and trigger the production of a special enzyme that causes you to remember Christmases in the past and smile a lot. They are food for the heart, the memory, and the spirit. Let there be no conversation about thighs and cholesterol.

The first Christmas cookie we ever met was Mrs. Schultz's butter cookie. Mrs. Schultz was the wife of the dean of Bluffton College, where Mom and Dad went to school, which means that this cookie has been in our family longer than we have. These were the most important of all our Christmas cookies, and we were given to understand that they were so very special because they were made with "real butter." In those lean years back in the fifties, butter was truly a luxury in our family. Margarine (which we called "oleo" in the Midwest) was what we spread on bread and cooked with. Except at Christmas. Then Mom bought butter and used it lavishly in Mrs. Schultz's butter cookies. We were properly awed, and ate the fragile, delicious, buttery result in tiny nibbles.

There is so much butter in Mrs. Schultz's butter cookies that the dough is a little difficult to handle. You aren't allowed to bully it, which is why Mom was always in charge of the rolling and cutting. (It helps to have a pastry cloth and a pastry sock for your rolling pin when making these cookies.) We decorated them with just a light sprinkling of green or red sugar. We didn't use much, because the cookies were too fragile.

Mrs. Schultz's Butter Cookies

Makes 3 to 4 dozen

1 ½ cups butter, softened
1 cup powdered sugar
2 egg yolks
2 cups all-purpose flour
1 tablespoon vanilla extract
Red or green sugar, if desired

Thoroughly mix all the ingredients, except the colored sugar, in a large bowl, stirring until all the flour is incorporated. Cover the bowl tightly with plastic wrap and chill at least 4 hours or overnight.

Preheat the oven to 325 degrees. Roll the dough out thin (⅛ to ¼ inch thick), cut into shapes, and quickly transfer to an ungreased baking sheet. Decorate with a light sprinkle of colored sugar, if desired. Bake for about 8 minutes, watching closely so they don't burn. Remove from the oven, cool for a minute on the sheet, then remove and cool completely on a wire rack.

A third truth about Christmas cookies is that yours are sensational and everybody else's are ho-hum. We've given and received many a cookie plate in our day, but it is clear that we like our own best. Take the cookie ball. Everybody has a recipe for these Christmas classics, and most of them are fancier: Butter Balls, Mexican Wedding Cakes, or Pecan Balls.

Even the commercial bakers are in on the act, and after Thanksgiving you can generally spot packages of powdered-sugar-covered horrors called Polyester Holiday Charms, or something like that, in the grocery store. Avoid these. Just because there's an elf on the package doesn't mean he works for Santa. Ours and only ours are Cookie Balls, and they are the best a Christmas cookie can be. Each little bomb of calories is so buttery that it shatters at the slightest touch, dusting powdered sugar down your chin and shirt front, so pop it into your mouth and eat it in one bite. Ah, yes.

Cookie Balls

Makes 2½–3 dozen cookies

1 cup butter, softened
4 tablespoons powdered sugar
2 cups finely chopped pecans
1 tablespoon vanilla extract
2 cups all-purpose flour
Powdered sugar

ream the butter and 4 tablespoons powdered sugar together until well blended. Add the remaining ingredients, and stir until all the flour is incorporated. Wrap dough in plastic wrap and chill for at least 3 hours or overnight.

Preheat the oven to 350 degrees. Make dough balls about the size of a small walnut, and place on an ungreased cookie sheet. Bake 10 minutes. *Do not brown.* Remove from heat, cool for a minute or two, then roll the cookie balls in powdered sugar until entirely covered. Cool on a wire rack.

One of our oldest cookie traditions is pfeffernusse. "Pfeffernusse," for the uninitiated, means "pepper nuts." *Pepper cookies?* Keep reading. They are drab, rock-hard, peppery, tiny, not very sweet, dust-colored little cookie bullets. And we adore them. Our grandmother made them for us for Christmas when we were little, and now that she is gone, Gary is the only one in the family to bake pfeffernusse. He and Marsha have a whole cookbook full of nothing but pfeffernusse recipes.

Grandma's pfeffernusse were thumb-size, but for reasons beyond our ken, our brother makes his really small. They are about the size of a pencil eraser. With the help of Holly Beth, who is now seven, Gary rolls out his cookie dough into a long thin rope and chops off hundreds of teensy cookies. Every year he fills bags full of pfeffernusse on Christmas afternoon and hands them around to the rest of us. We crunch them during the long drive back to our respective homes.

Why do we love them so? Because they remind us of our grandmother. Because they come out of our Mennonite heritage. Because they have real black pepper in them, which gives them a bite. Because Holly Beth helps Gary make them.

Gary's Pfeffernusse

Makes about 2 gallons of tiny cookies

1 cup softened butter or margarine
3 cups sugar
4 eggs
1 cup milk
A little salt
1 teaspoon cinnamon
1 teaspoon ground cloves
1 teaspoon nutmeg
1 teaspoon black pepper
3 teaspoons baking powder
About 10 cups all-purpose flour

Cream the butter and sugar together until fluffy. Add the eggs one at a time, beating well after each addition. Add the milk, and mix well. Add the salt, spices, and baking powder; mix well. Add about half the flour; mix well. Turn out onto a floured surface, add the rest of the flour to make a very stiff dough, and knead thoroughly.

Store the dough in a tightly covered container in the refrigerator at least overnight (4 or 5 days is better) to blend the spices. It will keep for months.

To prepare for baking, roll the dough into thin ropes. Gary makes his about the size of a pencil. Use enough flour while rolling to keep them from getting sticky. Slice the ropes into ¼-inch pieces.

Preheat the oven to 350 degrees. Fill an ungreased jelly roll pan with one layer of the cut pieces. Bake about 10 minutes. Remove from the oven, scrape the pieces into a paper bag, and shake thoroughly. (This separates any pfeffernusse that are stuck together.) Pour them back into the pan and bake another 5 to 7 minutes or until nicely browned.

At the other end of the spectrum are turtle bars—the Christmas cookie version of the candy classic. They have a crust on the bottom, then layers of pecans and caramel topped with melted chocolate. Heaven. We like this recipe (which a friend of Mom's clipped from a magazine and gave her about ten years ago) because they are rich and gooey as all get-out, and very easy to make. Being a bar cookie, they are much less labor intensive than molded or dropped cookies, and this recipe produces a big panful.

Turtle Bars

Makes about 3 dozen

2 cups all-purpose flour
1 cup firmly packed dark brown sugar
½ cup butter

Topping
⅔ cup butter
½ cup firmly packed brown sugar
1 cup chopped pecans
1 cup chocolate chips

Preheat the oven to 350 degrees. Lightly grease a 9 by 13-inch pan. For the cookie crust, mix together the flour and brown sugar. Cut in the butter until you have fine crumbs. Press into the prepared pan.

For the topping, place the butter and brown sugar in a saucepan, and cook over medium heat until thick and bubbly. Sprinkle the pecans over the cookie crust, and pour the caramelized butter-sugar mixture over them. Bake for 18 to 20 minutes, until all of the caramel bubbles. Remove from the oven and immediately place the chocolate chips on top of the hot caramel. Let stand a minute or two to melt, then swirl with a knife. Cut while slightly warm, and cool before removing from pan.

Turtle bars are so gooey and fabulous that they tend to overshadow less flashy Christmas cookie entries, like our dear old lebkuchen. This is a shame. Lebkuchen (which probably means "humble but yummy" in German) have

been in our family since the dawn of time, and it wouldn't be Christmas without them. Full of citron and almonds and honey, and covered with a little slick of lemon glaze, they are lovely with a cup of tea in the middle of the afternoon. Plus they freeze, they mail, and they comfort.

As predictably as the Salvation Army bell ringers and the shortening winter days, there will come a time in November when Mom will pick up a package of citron and a jar of honey and produce a batch of lebkuchen. She stores the cookies in a tightly covered box, with a slice of apple in the box to keep them moist and chewy while the flavors blend and turn wonderful. They will literally keep for two or three months, and only get better.

Lebkuchen

Makes 4 dozen

Dough
¾ cup firmly packed light brown sugar
1 egg
1 cup honey
1 teaspoon lemon juice
2 teaspoons grated lemon peel
2¾ cups all-purpose flour
½ teaspoon baking soda
½ teaspoon salt
1 teaspoon nutmeg
1 teaspoon cinnamon

1 teaspoon ground cloves
1 cup chopped citron
1 cup chopped blanched almonds

Glaze
1 cup powdered sugar, sifted
1½ tablespoons fresh lemon juice

Preheat the oven to 350 degrees. Grease a 15 by 10-inch jelly roll pan or rimmed cookie sheet.

For the dough: In a large bowl, beat together the brown sugar, egg, honey, lemon juice, and peel. In a separate bowl, mix together the flour, baking soda, salt, spices, citron, and almonds. Add 1 cup of the flour mixture to the honey mixture, and beat well. Gradually add in the remainder of the flour mixture, beating well. The dough will be very stiff. Butter your hands, and press the dough into the prepared pan. Bake for 20 minutes.

Stir together the ingredients for the glaze, and pour over the cookies as soon as they come out of the oven. Cool on a wire rack; then cut into squares. Store in an airtight container with a piece of apple to keep the cookies moist.

Some members of the family wouldn't touch a piece of citron with a barge pole. But the funny thing is, every one of us would throw a conniption fit if Mom hadn't made lebkuchen for Christmas. And that's what a Christmas cookie tradition is all about.

Giving

*But in a last word to the wise of these days let it be said that
of all who give gifts these two were the wisest. Of all who give
and receive gifts, such as they are wisest. Everywhere they are
the wisest. They are the magi.*

　　　　　　　　　　　　　　　—O. Henry,
　　　　　　　　　　　　　　　The Gift of the Magi

Giving is what makes Christmas the most wonderful
holiday of the year. Every pan of fresh-baked Christmas cookies from the oven, every Christmas card and jar
of homemade jelly, every quarter clinked into a Salvation
Army bucket, and every gluey and lopsided Christmas tree
ornament is a gift.

While the intensity of one's desire for Christmas presents
lessens every year as we grow up, it seems that the need
to give at Christmas grows stronger with each passing
year. Perhaps the older we get, the more we have to share.
Or could it be that as we grow older we get clumsier at
telling people we love them, and giving presents helps us
along?

Cherish what is dearest while you have it near you; and wait not until it is far away.

—Thomas Carlyle

When our grandmother was in her nineties, she worried a great deal about what to give her grandchildren for Christmas. She lived in a nursing home and didn't have a lot to spend. But with the help of her friend Miriam, she found the best things to give. One year she copied a verse of poetry in her beautiful old hand and framed it together with a photograph. And another time we each received a yellow looseleaf notebook, filled with her reflections and poems. There were memories of India, a story about her wedding day, and poems she'd written about each of us.

We made her a memory book ourselves one Christmas, just a year or two before she died. Each of us wrote down some favorite reminiscences of our time with her and Grandpa. Gary wrote poems, and we stuck in snapshots taken over the years. I think she turned that book's pages every day and showed it to every visitor.

Another year, Kath and Jim made Grandma a family calendar; all the birthdays and anniversaries were written in, and a different family photo accompanied every month. Memory presents are the best of all gifts for loved ones of any age, but especially for old people, to whom the past is often dearer than the present.

We gave Mom a memory present one Christmas about ten years ago. Her gift to us, every day of our growing-up years, was to read stories aloud. She had (and has) the best reading-aloud voice of anyone, and kept us spellbound for untold hours as stories unwound before us. The eight-year span in our ages meant that the little ones joined that charmed circle for the sheer joy of hearing her voice. Roo and I understood none of Dickens, Shakespeare, or Sir Walter Scott, but we listened raptly all the same. Very often she kept us entertained as we five sorted and folded baskets of clean laundry. As we neared the bottom of the baskets there would be a work slowdown, by tacit agreement, to keep the story going a little longer.

So we decided to thank her for it at Christmas. We brainstormed to remember some of the books she'd read to us—*Moccasin Trail, Little Women, Heidi*—then dug them out of the public library and picked passages to read aloud to *her*. She had to guess the book—and she did, every time.

Some of the gifts you were given as a child you carry with you into adulthood. When we were very small, Grandma made each of us a quilt for Christmas. The older kids got paisley cotton, and Roo and I each had a "snowflake blanket"—red flannel comforters tufted with white yarn snowflakes. At ages three and five, we would pad downstairs in our matching yellow footie pajamas, clutching our snowflake blankets, and sit in front of the Christmas tree and wonder. Roo kept her snowflake blanket, now thin and worn, the nap of the old flannel just about gone, and she *still* wraps herself up in it. And Mom still uses the older kids' paisley quilts on our beds when we come home for the holidays.

The success of the beloved snowflake blankets was so obvious that Grandma made one apiece for the oldest grandchildren, Gary and Marsha's kids, Erin and Nathan. Taking a leaf from Grandma's book, Karol got into the blanket business and made thickly stuffed, quilted "puffs" for Kath and me one year. The velvet and floral printed squares were embroidered together and lace- and ribbon-trimmed— Kath's in brown and blue, mine in green and rose.

I kept the tradition going with Christmas quilts for Katie and Holly Beth a year or so after Grandma died.

I had lots of cotton scraps in Christmassy prints because that was the year I made everybody bibbed Christmas aprons. (Come to think of it, Kathy still wears that apron, which is dear and loyal of her, considering that it is very homely.) I quilted Santa-printed and candy-cane-dotted squares and embroidered their names on them. And as I did, I thought about Grandma and knew that some of her was going into gifts for the little girls who never got to know her.

We all love to make presents, but what Roo really likes is to wrap them. She collects paper and ribbon throughout the year, then outdoes herself by spending literally weeks creating packages so awesome it's a shame to open them. They are reverently packed into huge boxes for the drive to Ames from Cincinnati, so as not to crush the handmade trim. Once home, they're placed in front of the tree, and we all take a tour of them to ooh and aah.

Roo's other unalterable Christmas tradition is the gift of homemade caramels. Roo is the only one in our family who makes them, and she hasn't missed a Christmas since she was a teenager. Oozing cream and butter, Roo's caramels are the Rolls-Royce of Christmas candy. They are truly a gift of love, as she has to stir the caramel goop, unstopping, for a good hour at least. But it's worth every second over the hot stove; these caramels are so tasty that they bring tears to the eyes. The recipe doubles beautifully, but Roo says something goes wrong when you triple it, so don't.

Roo's Caramels

Makes 2 pounds or 130–140 bite-sized candies

2 cups sugar
⅛ teaspoon salt
¼ cup butter
¾ cup light corn syrup
2 cups heavy cream, divided
2 tablespoons coffee liqueur

Butter an 8-inch square pan.
Combine the sugar, salt, butter, syrup, and 1 cup of the cream in a heavy pan. Dissolve over medium heat until the mixture comes to a full boil, stirring constantly. Gradually add the remaining cream, slowly so that the boiling does not stop. Continue stirring until the mixture reaches 250 degrees ("hard ball") on a candy thermometer. Remove from the heat and stir in the coffee liqueur. Cool in the prepared pan.

When the caramel is firm and cool, remove the whole block from the pan and cut into ½-inch strips; then cut each strip into bite-size pieces. Roll each piece in a small square of waxed paper, and twist the ends. (Don't use plastic wrap, or the candy will taste like it.)

When we were growing up, we each got just one Christmas present apiece from our parents — lovingly and carefully chosen. Other children might have had piles of gifts from their parents and Santa, but our way was better somehow: each one of us gave a present to everybody else in the family.

One year when she was about eight, Kathy was foraging in Mom's closet several months before Christmas and came across her and Karol's presents: teenage dolls about ten inches tall. Greatly exhilarated to have found out a Christmas secret, Kathy promptly told Karol, named her doll "Lynn," and commenced sewing clothes for her. But Kathy's cheekiness subsided when she saw Mom's hurt over the spoiled Christmas surprise she had planned for the girls. And that's how kids learn that parents have feelings and that a Christmas gift is more than a doll.

The five of us bought presents for each other and our parents about a week before Christmas. When we were really little, Dad and Mom gave Roo and me six dollars (for six presents) to spend at a dime store. I vividly remember roaming through Woolworth's until I found the perfect smelly bath oil for Kath and Karol and Mom. It was so perfect that four-year-old Roo had to buy them the same thing with *her* tiny stash.

From the time Kathy and Karol were about eleven and

eight years old, they took a bus by themselves to downtown Columbus, Ohio, for their annual Christmas shopping expedition at the Lazarus department store. They dressed in their Sunday clothes, because Mom had solemnly assured them that clerks would treat them nicer if they were smartly dressed. Every year they each brought back one beautiful Christmas ball for the tree and, grandly, a cream puff apiece for their envious and admiring younger brother and sisters.

When we were older and living in Iowa, all five of us kids shopped for Christmas together at the Merle Hay Mall in Des Moines. It wasn't a very big mall in those days, so we would plan elaborate shopping strategies to avoid running into the person whose gift we were buying. We broke into pairs and threesomes and scattered throughout the mall, with instructions to reconvene at the clock in an hour. The plans inevitably failed, and we came across each other in the act of present-buying. Shrieks, banishings, and furtive leaps behind the clothing racks ensued.

But making things was even more fun than shopping. When we were small, Karol sewed doll clothes and stuffed animals for Roo and me. One year she made small stuffed dolls with Ping-Pong ball heads and features drawn with felt-tip markers. Another time there were bunnies and bears made out of pastel angora socks. I asked Karol what her

favorite Christmas presents of all time were. The ones she loved the best were the ones she made for us in the mid-sixties. They were big rag dolls, which she worked on secretly for weeks down in the basement. They were about three feet high, with thick wool braids and striped pinafores, and named, for no good reason, Roweena and Helena.

When Roo was in grade school, Karol helped her create a gift box to house Dad's chess pieces. The box was wooden—a cigar box, most likely—which Karol and Roo stained, then lined with turquoise felt. Glued on the lid was a knight, lumpily molded from craft clay and lacquered with turquoise paint that never quite dried. It was a splendid thing, that chess box. But more splendid was the gift of Karol's time and patience in helping her little sister make a Christmas present for Dad.

Our kids like to make things too. They want to make *real* things, solid and useful, not just paper stuff! One Christmas Katie made sand-paintings-in-a-jar for everybody in the family. The sand was actually table salt, colored by rubbing little piles of it with colored chalk out in the middle of the driveway. Katie spooned layers of the colored salt into little jars, carefully tipping them as she went along to get waves and ripples, until the jars were completely full. She put a cotton ball on top of the salt to keep it from moving, then glued down the lids.

Trust us on sand-paintings-in-a-jar. They really work. We know. Katie made them. Such is not the case with fruit

pomanders, which are included in every Christmas craft book. Beware the clove-studded orange, which no adult can possibly make, much less a child. I have permanent indentations in my thumb from the year I grimly punched thousands of cloves into tough-skinned oranges and lemons. After hours of juicy effort, I produced three cloved pomanders, and carefully wrapped them up to give away at Christmas. The pomanders then quietly and thoroughly rotted and turned an evil color.

Another homemade Christmas present that *does* work is a picture soap. One of the pleasures of having kids — and for me, nieces and nephews — is that you get to do those wonderful little-kid Christmas crafts all over again. When Karol and Kath were young, they made these picture soaps, which they called, elegantly, "sachets." Mom and Roo and I kept the gifts for years in our underwear drawers.

Here's how to do it. You start with a bar of soap — the prettier and perfumier the better. (In the old days one could buy Sweetheart Soaps with raised decorations; the girls painted the soap's curlicues and flowery indentations with gold paint.) Next you glue on the front of the soap a little picture cut out of a Christmas card. (Magazine and newspaper pictures bleed and smear, so don't use them.) Then you melt paraffin — carefully, it's very flammable — in a clean coffee can set in simmering water. When the paraffin is melted, stick a long-handled fork into the back of the decorated soaps and lower them into the liquid paraffin to coat the front. And there it is: a picture soap! And you made it yourself!

> *The holly and the ivy,*
> *When they are both full grown,*
> *Of all the trees that are in the wood,*
> *The holly bears the crown.*
> —Traditional English carol

Every Christmas Mom makes her "holly wreaths." Mom was named for her mother, Holland Agnes, called Holly. Our grandmother died when Mom was born, in a cabin in Canada in 1922, but her Christmas name was passed on in the family. Today we have three generations of Hollys—Mom, me, and Gary and Marsha's daughter Holly Beth.

Mom thinks the name makes the Christmas season particularly ours, and every year she puts her imprimatur on sweet raised coffee rings which she gives away by the dozens. She saves us the best one for Christmas morning breakfast. The tops are decorated with white icing and green spearmint "holly leaves," with red-hots for berries. (Nobody eats the icky-tasting spearmint holly leaves, but they're required for effect.)

Mom's Holly Rings

Makes 3 coffee rings

Sweet Dough
2 packages dry granular yeast
½ cup lukewarm water
2 cups lukewarm milk
½ cup sugar
2 teaspoons salt
2 eggs
½ cup soft shortening
7–7½ cups sifted all-purpose flour

Filling
½ cup melted butter
1 cup raisins
1 cup sugar
1 cup chopped nuts

Glaze
1 cup powdered sugar
3 tablespoons heavy cream

Mix together yeast and water, soak for five minutes, and stir. Mix together milk, sugar, and salt. Stir in the softened yeast mixture. Stir in two eggs and ½ cup soft shortening. Mix in, first with spoon then with hands, 7 to 7½ cups of flour. Add the flour in two additions, using the amount necessary to make it easy to handle. Knead until smooth and elastic. Place the dough in a greased bowl, turning once to bring greased side up. Cover with damp cloth and let rise in warm, draft-free spot until double (1½ to 2 hours). Punch down. Let rise again until almost double (about 1 hour). After second rising, divide dough into three pieces. Cover and let rest 15 minutes so dough is easy to handle. Grease three large cookie sheets. Roll each piece of dough into a rectangle about 12 by 18 inches. Add the filling ingredients: first spread with the melted butter; then sprinkle with the raisins, nuts, and sugar. Roll up lengthwise and join the ends, placing each large circle on a prepared cookie sheet. Make large snips about ½ inch deep every 2 inches in the circle, and turn each section slightly to expose the filling. Let rise until doubled. Preheat the oven to 350 degrees. Bake for 25 minutes.

When the rings have cooled, stir together the powdered sugar and cream for the glaze. Pour glaze over each and decorate with green-spearmint jelly candies and red-hots to look like holly sprigs.

Roo, who was born on December 26, thinks that Mom showed a distinct lack of foresight when she used up the Christmas names (Holly and Karol) on her older sisters. But she was almost a Christmas baby, and we think she's darned lucky the folks decided on Ruth and not Mistletoe.

That must have been an awful Christmas for Mom, though she remembers it cheerfully. All the furniture and most of the dishes had been packed up for an impending move from Pandora, Ohio, to Columbus. Grandma was there to help her make a Christmas dinner and Mom was there to eat it with us, but shortly thereafter Dad took her off to the hospital. Less than twenty-four hours later they brought home Roo, who placidly ignored the bustle around her and slept in a dresser drawer. Then when the baby was three days old, Dad hitched a trailer to the car, the entire family piled in, and we moved to the big city.

Mother's gallant and nearly successful attempt to produce a baby for Christmas Day was perhaps above the call of duty. Nonetheless we firmly subscribe to the notion that the best Christmas presents are homemade. Like the wonderful Christmas that sister-in-law Marsha made each of the Burkhalters a stuffed *Winnie the Pooh* character. There was a Piglet in his little striped shirt for Karol, and a Kanga with Baby Roo in her front pocket for Roo, naturally. Mom got Winnie himself, and Tigger went to Kathy. But best of all was my Eeyore, who had a tail with a strip of Velcro on it (and Velcro on his rump) so the tail could be taken off and put back on again. (Kath thinks that Marsha matched the animals to each recipient's character, which is all well and good if you're Tigger.)

Roo and Larry's daughter Maren fell in love with Eeyore and appropriated him during a visit to Washington when she was two. I think it was the magic tail. Someday I hope to get him back, but just to be sure, I'm throwing broad hints in Marsha's direction about the abduction, and the possibility of an Eeyore clone.

This is my box, this is my box.
I never travel without my box.
In the third drawer,
in the third drawer . . .
Oh, little boy! Oh, little boy! . . .
In the third drawer I keep
licorice . . . licorice . . .
black, sweet licorice, black, sweet licorice.
Have some.

—Gian Carlo Menotti,
Amahl and the Night Visitors

Kathy's recently taken to making boxes for presents: big, beautiful Victorian hatboxes, covered with flowered chintz and lace-trimmed. You can put anything—licorice, even—in them. When Gary and Marsha's daughter Erin graduated from high school last year, Kath made her a gorgeous hatbox and filled it with our Christmas cream cheese cookie cutouts. (Erin loves those cookies so much that she eats dozens every Christmas.) Kathy and her daughter, Katie, made the graduation cookies in the shape of a "90" and lavishly frosted them in Erin's school's colors. It was the perfect gift. And here's how we know: it made Erin cry.

Cream Cheese Cookie Cutouts

Makes about 7 dozen

1 cup butter, softened
1 package (8 ounces) cream cheese, softened
1 cup granulated sugar
1 cup light brown sugar, packed
1 egg
1 teaspoon vanilla extract
1 teaspoon baking powder
3½ cups all-purpose flour
1½ cups ground almonds

Frosting

2 cups powdered sugar
¼ cup butter, softened
3 tablespoons heavy cream
¼ teaspoon almond extract, if desired

In a large mixing bowl, cream together the butter and cream cheese. Add the sugars; beat till fluffy. Add the egg and vanilla; beat well. Stir the baking powder into the flour, and add gradually to creamed mixture, stirring well. Add the ground nuts. Wrap in plastic wrap and chill overnight.

Preheat the oven to 375 degrees. Roll out the dough on a lightly floured surface to about ¼ inch thick (you can "flour" the surface with a mixture of flour and powdered sugar. Either way, a pastry cloth and a stocking for your rolling pin really help here). Cut with cookie cutters dipped in flour, and place on an ungreased cookie sheet.

Bake for 6 to 8 minutes, until lightly browned. Remove and cool on a wire rack.

Blend the frosting ingredients together in a food processor or electric mixer. Frost the cookies when they are cool. (Thin the frosting with extra cream if it thickens while spreading.)

Christmas cards are like little presents. Every Christmas we each make a pilgrimage to the big wicker basket next to the fireplace, where we keep the cards sent by those dear souls who still remember us despite the fact that we haven't sent one ourselves for years. There are the family newsletters that are so bad they're good, pictures of new babies, grinning in their Christmas nightsuits, and wonderfully earnest family groupings.

We made a Christmas card one year. It was in the late 1950s, I believe. Dad typed our family news in green ink in the shape of a Christmas tree, leaving round spaces (to simulate Christmas tree balls) for us each

to write our names in red ink. We all gathered around the dining room table, filling in our names, folding, stuffing, and sealing.

Before Roo and I were born, Dad carved a linoleum block print of our house in Pandora, Ohio, and made hand-stamped Christmas cards. The wonderful thing about Christmas is that ideas and gifts and projects get recycled and redone and remembered and refurbished. Roo found the old linoleum stamper about twenty-five years later while rummaging in the attic. She promptly made a print and framed it as a present for the folks.

People's food presents become a holiday fixture. It's very nice to depart from the usual cookie plate and give friends and family something special that nobody makes but you. Kathy's friend Ruth Ann makes lovely rich bread puddings to be given away with a serving of hard sauce. The proud recipients swank about, bragging of their bread puddings, and the rest of us wish Ruth Ann would make us one.

Ruth Ann's Bread Pudding

Serves 6

1½ cups milk
4 tablespoons butter
½ cup rum

2 eggs
½ cup sugar
¼ teaspoon salt
1 teaspoon cinnamon
3 cups soft bread cubes
½ cup raisins
Grated nutmeg

Preheat the oven to 350 degrees. Butter a baking dish.

Scald the milk (heat it until bubbles form around the edge), and add the butter and rum. Beat the eggs in a bowl with the sugar, and stir in the milk mixture, salt, and cinnamon.

Put the bread cubes and raisins in the prepared baking dish. Pour the milk mixture over, and stir gently. Sprinkle nutmeg on top. Place in a pan of hot water. Bake 40 to 45 minutes, or until a knife comes out clean. Serve warm or cold, with hard sauce.

Hard Sauce

½ cup butter, softened
2 cups sifted powdered sugar
2 tablespoons rum

Cream the butter, sugar, and rum together until smooth. Chill for at least 3 hours, until hard.

Kathy and Karol remember that when they were very young, Eileen Amstutz gave us potato doughnuts for Christmas. Eileen was Mom's special friend and our next-door neighbor in the early 1950s, when our family (with only two girls and a little boy then) lived in Pandora, Ohio. Eileen would bring over plates of doughnuts for our Christmas breakfast. After we moved, she would pack them into a big potato chip can and mail them to us for a Christmas present. Some of Eileen stays with the family; Roo (Ruth Eileen) was named for her.

In Iowa potato doughnuts were called "spudnuts," and there were special Spudnut shops that sold them. We liked those Spudnuts, though of course they didn't hold a candle to Eileen's. Fortunately Kathy still makes them. She taught me how when she visited Washington last year to huddle over the early drafts of this very book. (I wanted to be sure that mere mortals could concoct these potato wonders. I did, so you can.)

The first hurdle was to improvise a pastry cloth and tube for the rolling pin, as I didn't own the real thing at the time. The pastry cloth is essential — dusted with flour, of course — because potato doughnut dough is sticky. We jerry-rigged one from two tea towels: one taped across the bread board, the other wrapped and rubber-banded around the rolling pin. Then we rolled out the dough, cut it with doughnut cutters, and fried the doughnuts in oil, turning each one as soon as one side began to brown. The trick with these doughnuts is to keep turning them so they brown evenly and cook throughout. We alternated doughnuts with doughnut holes, rolling them in sugar while they were still hot and eating them while we cut and rolled and fried the rest of the doughnuts. Yum. Thank you, Eileen.

Eileen's Potato Doughnuts

Makes 6 dozen small doughnuts

2 cups mashed boiled potatoes, hot
1 tablespoon butter
2 cups sugar
3 eggs
6 cups all-purpose flour
1 teaspoon salt
½ teaspoon nutmeg
2 tablespoons baking powder
1 cup milk
Salad oil
Granulated sugar

While the mashed potatoes are still hot, beat in the butter and sugar. Allow to cool; then add the eggs, one at a time, beating well after each addition. Sift together the flour, salt, nutmeg, and baking powder. Add the dry ingredients to the potatoes, alternating with the milk, stirring with a wooden spoon until well mixed. Roll out on a pastry cloth or floured board to about ½ inch thick. Cut with doughnut cutters.

Pour 5 or 6 inches of oil into a large, deep saucepan, and heat to 365 to 370 degrees. Put a couple of doughnuts at a time into the oil, and turn them continuously until they are brown. Drain on paper towels. If desired, roll in granulated sugar while still hot.

Food and crafts are gifts of time, of attention, and of love. They fill your heart and home with Christmas when you make and give them. Gary's beef jerky fills your heart and home with garlic. Notice in the recipe below that you bake it in a barely warm oven with the door open—guaranteed to smell up your house with wonderful beef jerky perfume. Gary got this recipe from the wife of a navy buddy, who used to send beef jerky in "care packages" to her sailor husband. The navy delivered mail when they were out at sea by lowering great packages from a hovering helicopter. Gary says you could smell the beef jerky before you could see the helicopter.

Beef jerky is another one of those great things that we get only at Christmas. As with the pfeffernusse, Gary is the only one to make it, and there would be trouble if he didn't produce those greasy, strong-smelling little packages for us every year. It's great to nosh on when Christmas is over and you've got the winter blues. We think it cures the common cold as well.

Gary's Beef Jerky
50–60 dried pieces

Marinade
1 teaspoon liquid smoke
1¹/₃ teaspoons garlic powder
1¹/₃ teaspoons pepper
1 teaspoon Ac'cent (MSG), if desired
1 teaspoon onion powder
¹/₄ cup Worcestershire sauce
¹/₄ cup soy sauce

1¹/₂ pounds flank steak

Combine all the ingredients for the marinade. Semi-freeze the meat; then cut it into ⅛-inch strips *with* the grain. Marinate overnight.

Put a rack in a pan, and arrange the strips on it. Set oven for 130 degrees. Leave oven door slightly ajar. Bake for 12 hours.

In the wonderful O. Henry story "The Gift of the Magi," the pair of lovers each parted with what they most valued in order to give something to the other. Homemade presents are a gift of the thing many of us value most—our time— to make somebody happy. Maybe that makes all of us at least distant cousins to the magi.

Christmas Eve

The Oxen

Christmas Eve, and twelve of the clock.
    "Now they are all on their knees,"
An elder said as we sat in a flock
    By the embers in hearth side ease.

We pictured the meek mild creatures where
    they dwelt in their strawy pen,
Nor did it occur to one of us there
    To doubt they were kneeling then.

So fair a fancy few would weave
    In these years! Yet, I feel,
If someone said on Christmas Eve,
    "Come; see the oxen kneel,

In the lonely barton by yonder coomb
    Our childhood used to know,"
I should go with him in the gloom,
    Hoping it might be so.

                   —Thomas Hardy

Our first acquaintance with Hardy's Christmas Eve poem, "The Oxen," came when we heard it sung as a tenor solo. It was set to music by Ralph Vaughan Williams in his great Christmas cantata, *Hodie* ("This Day"). Dad conducted *Hodie* at Iowa State University in the mid-1970s, with Karol playing violin in the orchestra. Every year since, we've played a recording of it at Christmas.

Our Christmases have always been full of music, and we make a lot of it ourselves. We spend the afternoon before our big dinner on Christmas Eve singing and playing Christmas music. We can usually produce an approximation of four-part harmony for carols, accompanied by Dad on the viola. And Karol and Dad and I fake our way through a couple of movements of the Mendelssohn piano trios. The kids teach us new things, like the hand jive for "Up on the Housetop" (click click click). Jonny will sing us a solo or two, and last year Kath, Jim, and Katie did a six-hand piano version of "Silent Night."

Last year, sandwiched between viola duets and "Angels From the Realms of Glory" was a rowdy dance and mime routine by Nathan to the tune of "Rudolph the Red-Nosed Reindeer." Nathan taught the moves to Jonny, and the two of them tore up the family room impersonating reindeer. The fact that Nathan, a quiet teenager with a serious penchant for rock and roll, turns out to be a terrific mimic (and a flawless reindeer) is just one more piece of evidence that Christmas Eve is magic.

When we were very small, our grandmother gathered us around her piano and taught us the twelfth-century English carol called "The Friendly Beasts." The song derives from an age-old myth that tells of another miracle on Christmas Eve. This other miracle, quieter than the blazing star and the kings, occurred when the animals around the manger spoke aloud. "The Friendly Beasts" has verses for five animals: a donkey, a sheep, a camel, a cow, and a dove. We would each pick our favorite and sing the animal's song. We still try to sing it as grownups, but it is such a tender story and we're so sentimental that we get all choked up over it, and the kids have to pitch in and help us.

> *Thus every beast by some good spell*
> *In the stable dark was glad to tell*
> *Of the gift he gave Emmanuel,*
> *The gift he gave Emmanuel.*
>
> —Traditional carol

"Yes, but what about dinner?" some small person wants to know in the middle of all the music. "Later," we say, though of course we're all famished because we've been in a permanent bustle since we woke up, and nobody remembered lunch. So we sneak away from the piano to the kitchen to munch on Karol's stuffed mushrooms and Mom's blue cheese ball, until somebody hollers from the family room that we need an alto on "Joy to the World" and would you all come back in here, please?

Olive Blue Cheese Ball

Makes 2 cups

1 package (8 ounces) cream cheese,
softened
8 ounces blue cheese, crumbled
¼ cup butter, softened
⅔ cup well-drained chopped ripe olives
1 tablespoon minced chives
⅓ cup chopped walnuts

Blend the cream cheese, blue cheese, and butter together.
Stir in the olives and chives. Cover and chill for several
hours or until firm, for easier handling. Form into a ball
and chill thoroughly. Just before serving, sprinkle with the
chopped walnuts. Decorate the plate with parsley sprigs.

A couple of years ago, Dad and Gary and I attempted
to play Brahms' "Cradle Song of the Virgin," a lovely voice-
viola-piano arrangement of the fifteenth-century carol "Joseph Dearest, Joseph Mine." Gary practiced the vocal part
(singing the alto line in baritone) in Mason City, Iowa; I
hacked through the piano accompaniment in Washington;
and Dad worked up the viola part in Ames. The idea was
that when we got together it would all work out. We gave
it a go at a Christmas Eve performance for the family, but
Brahms' rhythmic complexities defeated Gary and me, and
it just came apart at the seams.

The following year, Karol revived the project and upped

the ante by committing the three of us to perform the "Cradle Song" at her Unitarian Fellowship in Ames on the Sunday before Christmas. (Recall, please, that we'd never gotten it right yet.) We three again practiced in our separate cities, then commenced rehearsals in Ames a few days before the performance. We worked at it for hours, with family wandering in and out of the piano room to check our progress.

And this time the magic happened.

The rhythms that didn't make sense when sung or played alone all of a sudden worked when we were three. Well, we gave the Unitarians our best. I like to think that if the sublime Mr. B. could have heard us across the centuries, he would have approved.

Our pickup Christmas ensembles remind me of the family musicales we held when we were kids. We all played something in those days—Kath and I were pianists, Gary played cello and Karol violin, and even little Roo had a pint-size violin. (Mom listened and kept the peace.) Dad transcribed some tunes for our motley ensemble and we actually performed a gig or two: we did the sinfonia from the Bach "Christmas Oratorio" at the Presbyterian church one Christmas, and "Clowns and Acrobats" from the *Nut-cracker Suite* someplace or other.

But mostly at Christmas there was singing. Dad conducted the adult choir at the Worthington, Ohio, Presbyterian church for many years, and we five kids sang in the junior choirs. And just in case we hadn't had our fill of carols, every Christmas our friends the Taylors gave a caroling party for choir families. Dozens of us clustered around the piano to sing carols in four-part harmony, and afterwards we ate mountains of cookies. It was one of the nicest things about Christmas.

When I moved from the Midwest to Washington, I really missed Christmas carols. I no longer sang in a church choir, and a pop version of "Little Drummer Boy" in elevators and department stores was almost worse than no carols at all. Needing an excuse to sing (and an occasion to unload the hundreds of chocolate bourbon balls I'd produced), I decided to revive the Taylors' famous party. John and I invited friends over to the house to sing carols with us, and now it's our tradition. Nearly a hundred friends and colleagues crowd into our Capitol Hill row house every year to sing Christmas carols. We make a joyful noise, and then everybody eats bourbon balls. Just like they're supposed to.

Chocolate Bourbon Balls
Makes 3 dozen

1 package (1 pound) Oreo cookies
1 package (8 ounces) candied red cherries,
* finely chopped*
1 cup finely chopped walnuts
1 package (6 ounces) semisweet
* chocolate chips*
3 tablespoons light corn syrup
½ cup bourbon
Sugar

In a food processor, crush the Oreos into very fine crumbs. Place the cookie crumbs in a mixing bowl and add the chopped cherries and walnuts.

Melt the chocolate chips in a double boiler over simmering water. Remove it from the heat, and add the corn syrup and bourbon, stirring until well mixed. Pour the chocolate mixture into the crumb mixture, and stir until all the particles are moistened. Let stand for 1 hour at room temperature. Shape into walnut-size balls, and roll in sugar.

To keep little people from perishing of anticipation on the night before Christmas, we took to exchanging gifts of Christmas tree ornaments on Christmas Eve. Katie gave us "picture pops" to hang on our Christmas trees—three or four popsicle sticks overlapped, glued together, and spray-painted white (like a snowflake, obviously), with her school

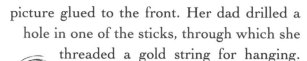

picture glued to the front. Her dad drilled a hole in one of the sticks, through which she threaded a gold string for hanging. Another year she produced pasta treasures — small pasta corkscrews, wheels, and elbows glued to heavy cardboard, painted gold, and hung from a ribbon. Now this isn't just loyalty: pasta treasures are very handsome, and you'd be awed and grateful if a little girl made one for *your* tree.

Roo once made really beautiful Christmas ornaments out of play clay. She cut little stars out of the pure white dough, dried them, sanded them smooth with an emery board, then airbrushed them with a can of air attached by a little nozzle to her design markers. She's an artist, so none of this was very daunting to her. But she promises that it's simple. An aerosol can of spray air, design markers, and special tips are readily available at art supply stores. Ordinary nonsoluble markers that you just scribble with work fine too, of course, but you can't spray with them.

To get stripes and designs, Roo stuck on little bits of masking tape before airbrushing with the markers. After applying the color, she lifted up the bits of masking tape, leaving bare stripes which she covered with powdered eye

shadow for shimmery, subtle colors. They are beautiful little stars, and have lasted for years.

We four sat around Mom's kitchen table one year and made ornaments from play clay the low-tech way. Roo'd left her sprayers at home, so we made do with paints and markers, glue and glitter. We gabbed, laughed, ate Christmas cookies, and made dozens of cookie-cutter shapes to hang on the tree.

Play Clay Ornaments

1 cup cornstarch
2 cups baking soda
1½ cups cold water

In a medium-size saucepan, combine the cornstarch and soda. Add the water all at once, and stir until smooth. Cook over medium heat, stirring constantly, until the mixture looks like dry mashed potatoes. Turn onto a plate, and cover with a damp cloth to cool. When the clay is cool, knead it with your hands until smooth and pliable. Roll it out thin (⅛ to ¼ inch thick), cut with cookie cutters, and poke a toothpick through the top to make a hanging hole. Air-dry the cutouts, turning frequently, so they dry evenly and don't curl. When nice and hard, sand with fine sandpaper or an emery board. Decorate with glitter or marking pens.

We've added another tradition to our Christmas Eve ritual. Karol and Jonny dug up some Christmas plays from the library, and we read through one on Christmas Eve. It was so much fun that we try to do one every year. We throw together costumes and a set (along the lines of ears pinned on stocking caps and gold foil stars stuck to the drapes) and read our parts from photocopied pages. Even the littlest kids can be part of the action in nonspeaking or ad-lib roles, and might be persuaded to sing a verse of "Frosty the Snowman" if you can work it into the plot.

Children love this kind of thing because they get to be part of something where the grownups are acting foolish. In one of our best plays, for example, Roo's husband, Larry, played the role of "King Conifer," a talking pine tree. He got the part because at six feet four, he's by far the tallest pine tree in the family. Larry won't be permitted to forget the performance anytime soon because, fortunately, Jim Lockard had the good sense to make a videotape of it.

Speaking of performing, my friend Christie Dailey's family has a marvelous tradition which grew out of the impos-

sibility of gathering their large and cheerful clan around the table all at the same time for Christmas Eve dinner. They commenced to divide up into two teams and eat dinner in two shifts, with one team serving the next. The thing developed into a full-fledged production, with servers serenading their patrons, improvising costumes, reciting poems, hiding little gifts under the napkins, and so on. We proposed this scheme to Mom last year, but she nixed it promptly. She thinks the Burkhalters are quite theatrical enough without encouraging more shenanigans at the Christmas Eve dinner table!

> *There were more dances, and there were forfeits, and more dances, and there was cake, and there was negus, and there was a great piece of Cold Roast, and there was a great piece of Cold Boiled, and there were mince-pies, and plenty of beer.*
>
> — Charles Dickens,
> *A Christmas Carol*

When we were young, we always had oyster stew on Christmas Eve—and on Christmas Eve only. Since it was almost impossible to get seafood in the Midwest, we considered oyster stew exotic and elegant. And we liked the fact that we could depend on it, every Christmas Eve.

To be quite honest, though, some of us like the tradition better than the thing itself. When we were kids we fished out the oyster swimmers—shudder—and plopped them into Mom's or Dad's bowl. These days we surreptitiously beach them on our salad plates. Once they're out, though, the broth is really tasty, and pretty to look at with its film of butter and flotilla of oyster crackers bobbing on the top.

Oyster Stew
Serves 4

2 cups milk
½ cup heavy cream
¼ cup butter
2 cups oysters, with liquid
Salt
Pepper
Paprika
Oyster crackers

Heat the milk and cream to scalding. In another saucepan, melt the butter, and add the oysters and liquid. Cook gently just until the oyster edges curl. Add them to the milk mixture, and season with salt, pepper, and paprika. Serve with oyster crackers.

Dessert is always Mom's fruitcake, a Christmas institution. It's dark and mysterious and liberally soaked in brandy. The grandkids won't touch it, but for those who have acquired the taste, Christmas Eve dinner would be unthinkable without it.

Now bring us some figgy pudding,
Now bring us some figgy pudding,
Now bring us some figgy pudding,
And bring some out here.

—Traditional English carol

One year Mom decided to vary things and attempted an English flaming figgy pudding. She steamed it just so, then unmolded it on a platter, doused it with brandy, and set the pudding aflame to bear in triumph to the table. But she got a bit reckless with the spirits. The thing was absolutely swimming in brandy, which sloshed, flaming, onto the lace tablecloth and began to burn merrily. There was much laughter and beating out of flames with napkins, while our grandmother, who at the age of eighty-five had never seen anyone try to set the dinner table on fire on Christmas Eve, softly said, "Oh my."

We've since abandoned steamed pudding immolation and stick to Mom's own figgy fruitcake, which, come to think of it, is so boozy it could spontaneously ignite, just sitting there.

Mom's Rich Figgy Fruitcake
Makes 2 loaves

3 cups sifted all-purpose flour
2 teaspoons baking powder
1 teaspoon salt
2 teaspoons cinnamon
½ teaspoon allspice
½ teaspoon ground cloves
½ teaspoon nutmeg
2 cups (1 pound) mixed candied fruit
  ("fruitcake mix")
½ cup candied pineapple, cut into thin
  wedges
1 cup (8 ounces) whole candied cherries
8 ounces light raisins
8 ounces dark raisins
1¼ cups (8 ounces) chopped dried Calymara
  figs, cut into pieces
2 cups chopped walnuts
4 eggs
1¾ cups firmly packed brown
  sugar
½ cup apple cider
½ cup brandy
¼ cup molasses
¾ cup melted butter
Whole candied cherries
Whole blanched almonds

Make this cake at least 6 weeks before Christmas so it can ripen. Preheat the oven to 275 degrees. Generously grease two loaf pans and line them with waxed paper or foil. Grease the liners.

Sift the flour with the baking powder, salt and spices into a large mixing bowl. Add the candied fruit, raisins, figs, and nuts, and mix well.

Beat the eggs until foamy. Gradually add the brown sugar, beating until light and fluffy. Blend in the cider, brandy, molasses, and butter. Add to the fruit mixture, and stir until well blended. Pour into the prepared pans.

Bake for 2½ to 3 hours, until a tester inserted into the center of the cake comes out clean. Cool. Remove from the pans. Remove liner paper. Wrap the cooled cakes in brandy-soaked cheesecloth; then wrap with foil. Will keep well for 6 months. Periodically remoisten the cheesecloth with brandy. Before serving, decorate the top with almonds and cherries.

After dessert, the littlest kids are packed, struggling, off to bed. Dad and the guys clean up the dishes, and the rest of us sit around the table for talk and jokes and just one more cookie. When the last slice of fruitcake is gone and the coffee has grown cold in our cups, we rouse ourselves to finish up our Christmas wrapping and sewing. Many is the time that one or the other of us has sewed doll dresses into the wee hours of the morning. The last project of all is to hang the little kids' stockings over the fireplace in the living room.

Now, about Santa. When we were little, our Christmases were so filled with stars, angels, grandparents, cookies, carols, kings-on-camel-back, and each other that there wasn't much room for Santa Claus. Moreover, gift giving at home was very precious, and we couldn't countenance the idea of crediting a mystical and whiskered stranger for the gifts we knew our family had chosen for us with love and care.

Kathy recalls only once having any thoughts about Santa Claus, when she was five years old. She knew that *her* presents came from Mom and Dad, but just to be safe, she listened hard for sleigh bells on Christmas Eve until she fell asleep. The rest of us were largely agnostic on the question of Santa, which got us into big trouble with adults who were true believers.

In about 1962, when we ranged in age from six to fourteen, we lived next door to a large family who promoted Santa ardently. Their entire Christmas revolved around keeping their youngest kids in the dark about who was really providing the presents. As a matter of fact, they even  tried to conceal what day Christmas was, so that they could smuggle in a tree late on Christmas Eve and surprise their darlings on Christmas morning. On the day before Christmas, one of us, wholly innocently, let slip that tomorrow was the big day, and speculated about what was under our tree from our parents. One thing led to another, and

before we knew it, the neighbor children had been more or less enlightened. Their mother was so mad that she didn't speak to us for weeks.

Having a little girl herself reignited Kathy's early fascination with sleigh bells on Christmas Eve. After Katie was born, Kathy couldn't resist embroidering a bunny stocking for her and putting out a plate of cookies and milk for Santa and the reindeer. At the same time, Kath and Jim made it quite clear that grownups who loved her were responsible for Katie's presents and that Santa was just for fun.

Eventually the rest of us capitulated and hung stockings for all the littler kids. (I always believed in the reindeer, anyway.) And that's how the chubby old sprite insinuated himself into our Santa-less family.

Christmas Morning

When we were young, Christmas morning before the presents were opened was the most delicious moment of the entire year. We were up with the birds. We prowled about the tree, poking things and guessing madly. The wait for our parents and grandparents to straggle in was unbearable, but finally they came, wearing their bathrobes and carrying cups of coffee.

They made us wait a little longer while Dad read the Christmas story. After all the excitement and bustle and bursting happiness of the days before Christmas, the reading of Luke's words by the tree suspended us for a moment in time. Did we stop breathing? It seemed so. We sat very quietly — even the smallest were still — while the ancient words flowed over us.

And they came with haste, and found Mary, and Joseph, and the babe lying in a manger. And when they had seen it, they made known abroad the saying which was told them concerning this child. And all they that heard it wondered at those things which were told them by the shepherds. But Mary kept all these things, and pondered them in her heart.

Luke 2:16–19

117

And so did we.

For a time, after we'd grown up and gone our separate spiritual ways, we substituted various readings for Luke's words on Christmas morning. Mom read a few short stories, like "Why the Chimes Rang" and "The Little Match Girl," and one year we each took a part and read the Christmas morning scene from *Little Women*.

But the substitutes never really worked. We missed the Christmas story, with its words worn silky smooth from constant use, the images and ideas connecting us to Christmases in the past. Now we're back to having Dad read the Christmas story, and as he reads, I can see us around the tree thirty-some years ago, with the littlest girls sitting on Grandpa's lap. And I can imagine that at Burkhalter Christmases many years from now, we'll have our own grandchildren in our laps. And as the Christmas story is read, we'll always hear it in Dad's voice.

And then it's time for presents, and the room fills up with ribbons and hugs. We take hours doing it, as each present is handed around and exclaimed over before the next one is opened. Jonny helps Grandpa carry presents to and fro, and toddlers frisk through the tidal waves of wrapping paper, while Larry remembers it for us with his camera.

Mom periodically disappears into the kitchen to put on another pot of coffee, or to frost the breakfast figure-eight rolls with maple icing. These are a special Christmas breakfast thing, made from the same sweet yeast dough she uses in her holly wreaths.

Christmas Morning Figure-Eights
Makes about 3 dozen

Sweet dough
2 packages dry granular yeast
½ cup lukewarm water
2 cups lukewarm milk
½ cup sugar
2 teaspoons salt
2 eggs
½ cup soft shortening
7–7½ cups sifted all-purpose flour

Maple glaze
2 cups powdered sugar
¼ to ⅓ cup heavy cream
½ teaspoon maple flavoring
Dash of salt

Mix together yeast and water, soak for five minutes, and stir. Mix together milk, sugar, and salt. Stir in the softened yeast mixture. Stir in two eggs and ½ cup soft shortening. Mix in first with spoon, then with hands, 7 to 7½ cups of flour. Add the flour in two additions, using the amount necessary to make it easy to handle. Knead until smooth and elastic. Place the dough in a greased bowl, turning once to bring the greased side up. Cover with a damp cloth and let rise in a warm, draft-free spot until double in bulk (1 to 1½ hours). Punch down. Let rise again until almost double (about 1 hour). Punch down again, and let rest 15 minutes. Grease several cookie sheets.

Pinch off a hunk of dough, and roll it until you get a rope about 10 inches long. Twist it into a figure-eight and pinch ends to seal. Repeat until you have used all the dough, placing the figure-eights 2 inches apart on the prepared sheets. Cover with a towel, and let rise until doubled, about 1 hour. Preheat the oven to 350 degrees. Bake for about 10 minutes.

To make maple glaze, whisk together all the ingredients until smooth. Spread on cooled figure-eights.

As the first parents among us kids, Gary and Marsha understood the essentials about children's presents sooner than we did. Marsh knew, for example, that for kids under five, the quantity of gifts under the tree matters *a lot* more than the quality. To prevent the Christmas morning phenomenon of woebegone three-year-olds with quivering chins querying, "Are there any more for me?" she wraps up dozens of little presents for our youngest kids: crayons, coloring books, doll clothes, stickers, and so on.

A great love goes here with a little gift.
— Theocritus

Marsh is particularly in tune with kid culture: she always gets the kids the perfect present. It would never have occurred to me that what a four-year-old most yearned for was a "Sparkle Pony." And Marsh was responsible for the first Barbie dolls and "Pound Puppies," while we were still imagining that kids liked those nice handmade wood pulltoys as much as grownups did.

Sparkle Ponies notwithstanding, though, one of the best presents I know of for a kid is an artist's box. Roo and I each got one from Grandma and Grandpa when we were about three and five years old. They were nice sturdy flat cardboard boxes with tight-fitting lids, and they were filled with art supplies: new crayons, stick-on gold stars, a paper punch, scissors (with rounded tips), a jar of glue, colored construction paper, and an "Ideal" Christmas magazine to cut pictures out of. We were enthralled.

Of all the gifts we received over the years, the art boxes were among our very favorites. So when Erin was little, Roo and I made her one. She told me fourteen years later that it was *her* favorite Christmas present of all time.

Kathy's favorite Christmas present was a Mennonite hymnal that Mom and Dad gave her when she was in the sixth grade. Kathy used it when she played piano for Sunday school class, and she uses it still for family Christmas caroling. It was an enormously important gift to a little girl who didn't get many new things. In those days, most of our clothes were hand-me-downs from friends, or used clothes from a Columbus thrift shop called the Trading Post. We littlest sisters loved the Trading Post; we thought the used clothes were wonderful. (We knew we certainly weren't going to get a *new* poodle skirt!) And Mom bought a couple of old frothy Trading Post formals for our dress-up box.

But by the time you are in the sixth grade, you need something made just for you. The Mennonite hymnal was all Kath's own. It was brand spanking new, and best of all, it had her name — Kathlynn Burkhalter — embossed in luxurious gold letters on its blue cover.

But the best gift we've given each other over the years is that we all come home, every Christmas. Roo and Larry made the trek from Cincinnati when Maren was six weeks old. They packed their car with the kind of baby paraphernalia that new parents think they must have, so John and I picked up their suitcases when we passed through Cincinnati on *our* trek west. The temperature was sub-zero.

Halfway home to Ames, to Roo's horror and amazement, the baby overflowed in her little car seat, completely drenching herself and everything else. (You know the way babies do. One minute they're fine, the next minute it's like a science fiction movie.) Roo and Larry pulled off the highway at a filling station, stripped Maren to the skin, and mopped her up. And then they discovered that they had not one tiny baby suit to put on their newborn because their suitcases were tooling down the highway several states behind them.

They piled her with coats and baby blankets and drove on in to Ames. Maren, by this time, was happy as a clam, but Roo and Larry were in agony. What should have been the triumphant arrival of proud new parents at the ancestral home was in fact an embarrassed slink through the back door, bearing the infant naked as a jaybird. We loved Maren anyway, of course. And Mom, bless her, had the presence of mind *not* to suggest to the new mother that it is customary to clothe a baby in the dead of winter.

We'd go through fire and water to get home at Christmas, but we didn't know till last year how much it meant to our kids. That year must have been a very hard Christmas for Jonathan. He was ten years old, and it was the first Christmas after Karol and Ted's divorce. Jonny knew he would be seeing his Dad later during the holidays, but it wouldn't be with our whole gang. Jonny missed him, and so did we.

The Sunday before Christmas, we went to the service at Karol and Jonny's Unitarian fellowship. It is the custom there for people to come forward, light a candle, and tell the group what they are thinking of, worried about, or thankful for. One after another, grownups and college students walked to the front of the room. There were graduations to report, illnesses to mourn, and babies to celebrate — a dozen candles were lit. Then a blond, ten-year-old boy came forward. He lit a candle and said, "I just want to thank my family for coming home for Christmas." And the whole row of us turned into a collective grin, ear-to-ear. Jonny's family. That's us.

When the last present is unwrapped and the family room is dug out from under the paper and ribbons, we go in to breakfast. Christmas breakfast is hearty, because it is the big meal of our Christmas day. There will be coffee and screwdrivers, fruit salad, a big egg casserole, and platters of sweet rolls, to the bursting point.

Karol made up a terrific apple breakfast thing last year, and it was so good we declared it a tradition after the first bite. Here's how to make it. First you have to coerce some-

one into peeling about a dozen medium-size tart apples. (Gary and I had a loud and boisterous race to see if his eccentric method of taking the skin off the entire apple and then slicing and coring it was faster than my conventional approach of cutting

them into sections and *then* skinning and peeling them. The peels flew and there was a certain amount of yelping and elbowing, and Gary emerged the victor. Until next year.)

Next you dice and fry up about a pound of bacon till crisp, then add the apples, a cup of brown sugar, and a tablespoon of cinnamon, and stir the whole business over low heat until the apples get soft and wonderful.

After breakfast we make another admiring tour of all the presents and launch a search for the pair of Christmas earrings that has vanished into the wrapping paper twilight zone. The youngest kids inevitably and immediately strip their new dolls naked, and scatter small parts from their Christmas games so that some stocking-footed adult will step on one and shriek. New sweaters are pulled on over pajamas and modeled. A Ping-Pong match ensues in the basement, and the recordings we've given each other are on the stereo.

And so the day slips into afternoon. There will be sledding or tromping in the woods, a fire in the fireplace, a game of cards, and a bowl of soup. But much too soon the day is gone. Gary and Marsha and their kids pack up for the drive to Marsha's folks in northern Iowa, and John and I head out for Ohio, where we'll see his family. Mom and Dad and the others—a smaller, quieter group now—linger by the fire and retell every detail of another memorable family Christmas.

And so we say goodbye.

Afterword

That's our family at Christmas. But you know, all this fun didn't happen automatically. A couple of years ago, we sisters sat down and decided that we wanted more out of Christmas. As we took down our trees after the holidays, we had the sinking suspicion that Christmas wasn't everything we had hoped it would be. We wanted to play more. We wanted to enjoy the kids and our parents and our brother and each other more. We wanted to get a huge bang out of cookie cutouts and "Frosty the Snowman." We wanted to sing more, and remember more. We wanted it to be the way it was when we were kids.

So we resurrected old traditions and brought in some new ones. We made the food easier so we could sit around and gab longer. We planned more activities for kids and grownups together, like the Christmas play, sledding parties, and a musical whoop-de-doo for Christmas Eve. And we made a bigger fuss out of traditions, in the hopes that the kids will flip if anything is missing next year.

But more than anything else, we four sisters got to know each other better. In the course of planning more fun for Christmas, we spent more time on the phone and visited

each other more often. We shared more recipes and crafts and party ideas, and found ourselves sharing more happiness and sorrows and successes, too. Christmas made us closer, and that made Christmas better.

Thus along about August, the telephone calls between Ames and Cincinnati and Sycamore and Washington start to pick up. Without even realizing it, we're mentally making Christmas party menus and we're keeping an eagle eye out for presents. By September we're clipping recipes for winter stews and pies and cookies. We find ourselves fingering a bolt of Santa cloth at the fabric store, and mooning over the early editions of holiday women's magazines. October finds us planning our sisters' Christmas shopping reunion, and November is a blur of baking, freezing, canning, and sewing.

Before you know it, it's Christmas. And the cookies and ornaments and memories of all those past Christmases come crowding back as our thoughts wing home ahead of us. We pack up our cars with beribboned packages, fill thermoses with coffee and lunch bags with cookies, and throw snow shovels in our trunks for the long, wintry drive home to Iowa.

And as we round the corner to Mom and Dad's, there is a big paper star glowing from the upstairs window. It looks happy to see us.

Index of Recipes